Lost Creek Books presents
Wesley Murphey's books—

Fiction

Trouble at Puma Creek: A Vietnam vet, a Deadly hunt

While hunting deer in Oregon's Fall Creek Forest in 1980, Vietnam veteran Roger Bruington is murdered by an Oregon State Police officer after discovering a suspicious shack. Did finding the shack get him killed? Or was this a government hit because Bruington was finally going to reveal the U.S. Government's cover up of the evidence he turned over in 1974 proving American POWs were still being held captive in southeast Asia a year after all POWs were supposedly released? (338 pages)

A Homeless Man's Burden

Based on the actual still-unsolved 1960 bean-field murder of little *Alice Lee* near Pleasant Hill and Dexter, Oregon. Wesley Murphey picked in that very field for many years and, as a teen, worked for Alice's father. Murphey's father was Alice's school bus driver and the mail carrier in the area for 25 years. This somewhat autobiographical story begins on the McKenzie River in 2010 with a dying homeless man's partial confession. (302 pages)

Girl Too Popular

Being the most popular girl in town is not all it's cracked up to be—Carly Cantwell finds out why when she is kidnapped to a remote location in the forest. Is her abductor connected to her ex-stepfather who she rejected? Or is someone or something greater at work here? (178 pages)

To Kill a Mother in Law

When Dan Thurmond married Brenda, he got Maureen Muldano, the mother in law from hell. Now, with his marriage on the rocks, and shut out by his wife's restraining order, Dan's hypocritical, pseudo-spiritual, controlling mother-in-law and other wolves in her family are going to reap what they sowed. (302 pages)

Nonfiction:

Blacktail Deer Hunting Adventures (Revised 2013 available 8-2013)

A classic. The only true adventure account ever written on hunting the Pacific Coast's blacktail deer. Well Illustrated. "Anyone who has ever hunted blacktail deer can relate to this book and can gain some good hunting lore from reading it." -- Boyd Iverson author of Blacktail Trophy Tactics (180 pages)

Conibear Beaver Trapping in Open Water

Master Beaver Trapping Techniques. Recognized as one of the top beaver trapping books in America. 110 illustrations. (110 pages)

Trap Otters, Beavers, Raccoons, Nutrias & other critters (avail 8-2013)

Trapping techniques for these furbearers by veteran trapper Wesley Murphey. Includes numerous published articles, lots of supplementary information, along with lots of photos and drawings. Many situations and sets described and well illustrated. (110 plus pages)

Fish, Hunt & Trap a Little (Three Volumes)

Volumes One and Two (180 pages, and over 60 illustrations in each)

True Tales and Tactics by Wesley Murphey and his deceased father, Don Murphey. These volumes include many articles previously published in national and regional publications—and many great never-before-published articles that will charm you, teach you, entertain you, make you laugh and remember when, and inspire you to get out into the great outdoors to fish, hunt and maybe even trap a little.

Volume Three to be released in April 2014.

See and order all Wesley Murphey books at lostcreekbooks.com

FISH, HUNT
and TRAP a LITTLE

(Volume Two)

True Tales and Tactics

Wesley Murphey
and **Don Murphey**

Lost Creek Books
La Pine, Oregon

Fish, Hunt and Trap a Little (Volume Two)

Published by Lost Creek Books, La Pine, Oregon
http:lostcreekbooks.com

Cover Design: Howard Rooks Graphic Design, Pleasant Hill, OR
Cover Photo: Murphey boys and friend, crappies, Fern Ridge, 1962
(Photo by Don Murphey)

Poems: By Karl Keen (Poems of the Mountain Man)
and Ross Turner were used with permission.

ISBN 978-09641320-9-2
Library of Congress   2013936391   (Volume Two)

Printed in the United States of America by Sheridan Books

Outdoor True Adventure
Fishing and Hunting True Adventure
Fishing Tactics

Volume Two

Contents

I dedicate this book to the co-author, my dad, Don Murphey, who taught me so many wonderful things. Thanks, Dad. I love you!
Wesley

The Murphey twins both home on leave from the Navy, Oct 1975.
(From left) Rob, Grandma Rodenberger, Don Murphey, and Wes.
Rob is stationed on the diesel submarine USS Bonefish SS 582.
Wes is on his way to submarine school, then to USS Guardfish SSN 612.

Introduction

I've been told many times that I was born 100 years too late. In fact, I believe I was probably born 150 years too late. Had I been born in 1807 instead of 1957 I would have been one of the mountain men who trapped, lived off the land and explored many new territories, while never being satisfied to stay at one job for very long. The mountain man kinship-with-nature is in my blood in a way that I'm not sure it ever has been with anyone else in my family, except for my dad, Don Murphey—the co-author of these three *Fish, Hunt and Trap a Little* volumes. I know Dad shared many of the same dreams I had of trapping, fishing and writing full-time.

Many people would say he was more responsible than I've been. And they are undoubtedly right. He worked for 25 years as a U.S. Mail carrier in the Dexter-Lost Creek area, while often holding down a second job as a bus driver, shingle packer or meat cutter. Me, I've never stayed at one job more than two years. I have, however, worked for the same employer four different times for up to a year and a half at a time.

My biggest problem was that I liked being my own boss, and I loved fur trapping. So when late-fall approached, I'd usually find a way to be free from a regular job in order to trap. Many of my

1

trapper friends can appreciate that about me, although some of them kept a regular job while trapping as much as they could on the side.

Even though I've caught thousands of animals in my traps, if I was to sit down and figure out my hourly wages for all the years I trapped full-time, it would have been less than minimum wage. During the winter trapping season, between checking traps and handling fur, I often put in twelve-to-fourteen hour and sometimes longer days six days a week, and put in several hours on Sundays as well. Only a fool does that for such little payment. I've been criticized by some for not "getting up to an alarm clock every day"— like they do—in order to go work on an employer's or supervisor's terms, deal with his/her or other people's varying moods, expectations or pressures down at the office, store, mill, warehouse or some other traditional place of employment.

The payment I received may not have amounted to a lot monetarily, true. But the mental and physical stimulation, enjoyment and satisfaction I gained by spending countless hours in the wild on my trapline, on my own terms, without the stress of meeting someone else's demands and expectations, are hard to put a value on. When I add in all the time I've spent camping, fishing, hunting, mushroom picking and hiking, plus getting to write about many of those experiences, I can honestly say I've lived my dream for a fair part of my adult life. How many of you, doing traditional jobs, can say the same thing? Oh, many people have bigger houses, trucks and toys, but at what price?

As you read Dad's and my outdoor stories, and the few poems I've borrowed from two other outdoor lovers, put the worries of your job or life aside for a little bit. When you're done reading, find a way to get out into God's wonderful outdoors with your family or a friend or two to fish and hunt and maybe even trap a little. Trust me it will be medicine to your soul and great for your stress level.

Kids, Cats and Waterdogs

Wesley Murphey

Upon reaching the little inlet to fish at Lookout Point Reservoir, southeast of Lowell, Oregon, we picked out some flat rocks to use as seats. I cut a couple of forked, green willow-shoots to use as stands for our two fishing rods, shoved them into the mud, then lit the lantern as darkness fell upon us. Cody (5 ½) and Tasha (3 ½) settled in close to me. The "cats" we were after were actually bull-heads, miniature cousins to big catfish.

Shortly after dark, there was a jerk on the left rod tip. "There's a hit," I said. "You get the first one tonight, Cody."

Immediately I released the reel's button to allow the fish to free-ly take the worm and hook. After twenty seconds, I reeled up the slack from the line and upon feeling the fish, I set the hook. Cody was already grabbing the rod as I positioned myself behind him. The fish tugged valiantly on the line but in less than a minute was at water's edge. Cody and I lifted it out of the water by raising the rod tip toward the stars. I grabbed the line and brought the floundering fish close to Cody who cautiously reached out to feel it.

"It's a big one, Dad!"

"Good going, Cody," Tasha said.

Wes and the girls, daughter Tasha, 6, (in back) and friend Heather, 5, with a catfish at Lookout Point Reservoir in 1996.

I then placed the chubby eleven-inch yellow bullhead into our metal bucket. As I re-baited and cast the line, the kids shined the flashlight into the bucket to admire their prize. Cody, wanting to see with his hands (he has very little vision), reached in and carefully felt the fish; he had been pricked on a couple other occasions by the sharp spines on the end of a catfish's dorsal and pectoral fins.

The kids stayed busy with the bucket and fish while I re-baited, cast the worm out and then watched hopefully for another strike. Ten minutes later it came, again on the left rod. Following the same sequence as before, I helped Tasha hold the rod, and reel in her fish. She couldn't stand still, as we lifted the fish from the water.

"I got a big one, Cody!"

"Way to go, Tasha," he said, as he crowded in close and patted her on the back.

I then placed the fish in the pail next to Cody's. After thoroughly examining the fish with both hands, Cody said, "Mine's a little bigger than yours."

Tasha pointed the flashlight into the bucket to look closely at the two cats. "Yours *is* bigger, Cody."

With that settled and both kids thrilled at their skilful fishing, I continued waiting for the next bite.

Fifteen minutes passed, and then there was a slight tug on the right rod tip.

"It's my turn," Cody said, making ready to receive the rod.

When I set the hook, I didn't get the strong response I'd hoped for. Still I handed the pole to Cody who feverishly worked the reel. In the past, a light reply on the end of the line meant we either had a sculpin-minnow, a very young catfish, or ...

"You caught a waterdog," I said, disgustedly, as Cody hoisted the rod tip. In came a brown-backed, orange-bellied salamander about seven or eight inches long.

"I want it," both kids said almost simultaneously, already familiar with "dogs" from previous catfishing trips.

I wasted no time separating the waterdog from the worm hanging from its mouth and handed the dog to the kids. I need not have been in such a hurry to re-bait and cast, because the remaining hour and a half of fishing netted us only one more catfish, a big disappointment to me, especially since I spent that time reeling in and removing one waterdog after another. The kids didn't mind; they had a great time playing with the waterdogs.

When it was time to go home, I let the kids each bring one waterdog with them. At home we put the dogs in a water-filled 10 gallon aquarium with some rocks, leaves, twigs, and a small piece of floating driftwood. We fed them worms and live minnows, and kept them for almost a year. The kids and their friends loved watch-

Waterdog — an Oregon Newt

ing, and playing with, their waterdogs almost daily. We eventually had to replace them with a new set of 'dogs.

"Waterdogs" are abundant throughout much of the west coast. The rough-skinned Newt—the most prevalent species of salamander in western Oregon and one of the largest—can be found from sea-level at the coast to the top of the Cascade Mountains. I've found them in every pot-hole and high mountain lake I've been to.

According to *The Oregon Encyclopedia*, the newt's range extends from southeast Alaska to central California. Besides their prevalence in water bodies, adults also roam and forage by day and night in nearby forests and grasslands, feeding on invertebrates like worms, spiders and various insects.

My first exposure to waterdogs came when my twin brother, my next-older sister and I—all pre-schoolers—were on a fishing trip with Dad at Dexter Lake a couple miles or so below Lookout Point Dam. Dad was down at the water fishing and the three of us were playing in the forest about forty yards above him, when my sister Becky cried,

"An alligator!"

Waterdog in Murpheys' aquarium.

In terror we ran down to Dad at the water and clung to him warning him of the baby alligator that was crawling down the hill. We scanned the woods around us fearing the baby's parents might be nearby. Dad knew immediately that Becky had seen her first waterdog.

He took the three of us back up the hill and, upon finding Becky's "alligator," picked it up without hesitation and held it in his palm.

"There aren't any alligators around here," he said. "This is a full-grown waterdog salamander. It won't hurt you. They're actually fun to play with."

He then took our fingers and helped us rub its smooth belly and rough back. From then on when we went on an outdoor excursion with Dad we would find some waterdogs and make them our playmates. Somewhere between being a young child and becoming a parent, I forgot how much fun waterdogs could be.

Which waterdog is the real one? Can you figure out what it's doing?

Those early catfishing trips with my kids taught me a valuable lesson about parenting: Provide the outdoor setting and then follow the kids' lead, being willing to forget my own agenda. If the catfish were biting—great. But if something else, like waterdogs, captured the kids' attention instead, that was fine too.

We often got to the lake an hour or more before dark so we could roam the shoreline looking for various treasures and get the materials we needed for a campfire. Hotdogs, buns and marshmallows routinely found their way into the pack too.

Editor's note: A waterdog's skin contains a toxin which protects it from predators. You should avoid hand to mouth contact, and wash your hands, after playing with one just as you should after handling a pet bird, rat, hamster or any other animal.

Beaver Time 1960-61

Don Murphey

When Dwight Stevens of Dexter, Oregon broached the idea of a part-time beaver trap-line, I couldn't give an on-the-spot answer. The idea had to soak me up a little at a time. A couple of weeks passed as I considered that I didn't have much "part-time" to spare in between driving both a U.S. Mail route and a local school bus.

"I remember how I used to travel your trap-line with you," Dwight had said. "What a thrill it was when we brought up a beaver on that drowning wire."

"You mean you could stand a few more of those thrills?" I answered.

"Sure could. And I want to learn about skinning and fleshing, marketing—all of it. I never paid much attention to that part during those earlier years."

A lot of trapping talk followed that first conversation—the kind that sets your pulse beating faster and then lingers on in your mind as you try to go about your normal routine… until when beaver time rolls around you find your coils of wire are ready, your traps are laid out alongside your plans, and you have a partner that can no longer contain himself.

We chose the Christmas holidays as our beginning date. While mail is heavy, I was at least on vacation from the school bus; and Dwight's swing-shift job in the plywood mill wouldn't prevent him from arising plenty early to manage a trap-line. Though beaver season always opens with the general season in Oregon, November 15th, past experience has taught me to forget about "getting my share" and begin only after beaver are approaching the prime state. There's no sense in getting half-price for your furs.

In western Oregon there is seldom much ice. We planned on working the valley of one of the tributaries to the upper Willamette River with its numerous feeder streams. The main vein of this small watershed is a creek that averages 30 to 40 feet wide during winter. Some of its feeders, though, are mere trickles in summer, one or two going completely dry in the lower reaches.

The Murphey twins, Robin and Wesley, with their dad's
55 pound superblanket beaver 1961.

Bill Murphey watching Dwight Stevens set a beaver trap 1960-61.

One of the more difficult aspects of working these small streams is finding a place to make a sure drowning set. More than likely the natural place to put in a trap will not encompass any deep water at all. Rarely do you find the perfect setting: deep water, fresh cuttings, and a beaver slide that enters the water at that desired low angle of descent. So sometimes you'll make a man-made slide giving it every possible native look. Maybe you'll add an artificial beaver mound by scooping up a few handfuls of mud from bottom and piling it nearby, thus making it possible to set your trap near the deep water you need.

Another thing you run up against on small streams that you hardly ever confront on bigger water is disturbing the beaver colonies. Just think— you must walk up and down the banks in order to find, make and maintain your sets, and inside these same banks are your beavers, feeling the vibrations of your footsteps and perhaps hearing your voice. These beavers are easily frightened away, going far upstream or down where they apparently use an old den until they feel it's safe to return. They do come back, of course, but you often have to wait a week or longer before taking that first animal. Caution is definitely the by-word on the small streams.

At the first set, Dwight was gathering rocks for the gunny sack that would be the drowning weight, while I measured off the necessary wire and straightened it. I fastened the wire to the weighted sack just above the rocks and then slipped the metal drowning slide, that was fastened to the trap's chain, onto the slide wire so that the only direction a trapped beaver could go was down the wire to the sunken weight. I then twisted the shore end of the wire to a handy root and tossed the weight out into deep water. Then I placed the trap in about eight inches of water, and placed a guide stick or two to force the beaver over the trap, and then laid some fresh cottonwood cuttings on the shore as bait. When this was done Dwight said, "Didn't you used to put some kind of scent at the set?"

"Yes," I answered, "but we have none. We'll have to catch a beaver first; shucks the first time around the line you'll have a beaver and we'll be rolling in scent."

"Can't you buy scent?" he persisted.

"Should have, probably, but it'd take several days to get now. Don't worry; we'll have a beaver right off."

Most of the beavers on the larger creek did not build dams, so our sets were made at fresh cuttings or at slides coming down from the banks. Knowing the location of dens is a highly important twist on such creeks as this because beavers will use an old den hole rather than go to all the work of digging out a new one, provided there is ample food supply nearby.   So if we came into an area where I knew there were old dens, we made a set, even if there was no sign evident. I've caught many a single old male beaver by doing this.

In several miles of creek we found only two dams and these were on backwaters. At each of them we made a setting where the animals had been crossing over the dam—one of my favorite sets. Deep water for drowning is always handy there.

Narrow passages where beavers have been traveling up or downstream are another kind of place I always look for, but you don't find many. We had one. An old log jutted out from under a drift at right angles to the main current and reached out to midstream. Two feet off the end of this a three-foot-thick cottonwood grew up on what once had been the stream bank but was now an underwater sand-bar. Our trap was laid between the old log's end and the tree on a sand bottom about ten inches deep. As the water rose we merely built up the bottom there and re-laid the trap. We stapled one end of the drowning wire to the cottonwood and tossed the weight downstream into deep water. This natural set made good contact on beaver for us.

When we had finished we had out what I considered twelve good sets, my motley collection of no. 4 long springs. Later, we had to change some of those first sets, as the water raised or lowered, or as we should find a more likely location.

The weather turned cold then and the stream fell. Dwight made the rounds on the second day, and again on the fourth and sixth days, and we caught raccoons. Every 'coon in the valley was abroad on those cold moonlit nights, I believe, but we caught not a single beaver.

Don Murphey with a big beaver, 1960-61.

"What's wrong?" Dwight kept asking, and there was one beaver trapper making with ready excuses. Fishermen are pikers at excuse-making compared to trappers. The chips were down when after ten days no beaver had been caught, and in order to save my soul I knew that one had better be caught pretty soon.

"Not moving," I'd told Dwight. "There are those kinds of nights, you know." But I felt Dwight wasn't convinced and I knew I wasn't; so I rummaged around in my shop until I found an old dry beaver castor gland. There had been plenty of time to obtain lure after all, I was thinking; no one should start a season without it.

I took that dry castor and worked on it with a wood rasp until I had a pile of granulated particles on a newspaper. It smelled pretty strong yet, though it was at least two years old. I poured the contents into a small medicine bottle that was half full of glycerine, and then I drove up the valley and went over the whole trap-line dabbing a little of my improvised scent at each set, moving the traps deeper or shallower as the water level dictated.

The next day, I was in the post office when Dwight drove up after finishing the line. "Come on out," he yelled. "I've got something to show you."

As I neared the open door of Dwight's sedan, it looked as if the back seat were full of beaver. He had two blankets (XXL), a large, and an extra large stacked in there, and you couldn't have wiped the smile from his face with anything short of steel wool. Confidence and excitement radiated from him as he told me which sets had paid off. Right then I was thinking I'd partially vindicated myself as a beaver trapper.

Now we had to go to work in earnest; the beaver were coming in. The fleshing and drying, and most of the skinning were done at my place where I had plywood sheets to nail the pelts out on. Later Dwight fell to skinning them at his place and dropping the pelts off on his way to work. I'd tackle the fleshing and nailing out in the evening after all other work was done for the day. Quite a bit easier, I remember thinking, than one man doing it all—though I missed a lot of the thrills of running the line. Most week-ends, however, I was with Dwight brushing up the sets or else moving traps.

One day Dwight came in telling of a man at his job who knew a farmer with a chronic beaver problem. He said the farmer would be tickled pink if a good beaver trapper moved in and cut down the population a bit, having long given up the idea of getting rid of the beaver tribe permanently.

"A couple of local young trappers tried to trap some of them a year ago, I understand," Dwight said, "but they didn't catch anything. The beaver have built several dams on this small creek and have caused the water to overflow into the farmer's pasture making a deep gulley and eroding his land in half."

"Sounds like we might help him and ourselves, too," I told Dwight. "But it'll be your project, pal. I wouldn't have enough spare time to go that far away to help you out."

Dwight went over with the three traps we decided we could spare and set it up. The farmer, Ronald Durflinger of Lynx Hollow, near Creswell, was truly glad to have him come in and obtained permission for us on the two bordering lands, also. Dwight told me, "The only thing is, I haven't yet caught a beaver entirely on my own. Don't know if I've got the stuff."

"This is your chance to prove you have," I assured him.

Two evenings later there was a phone call from Dwight. "I'll be bringing in a couple of beavers from Lynx Hollow Creek tonight on my way home from work. One of them weighs 43 ½ pounds; the other might make a large."

Then the next evening: "We got a medium from Lynx Hollow today. I'll drop the pelt off on my way to work tomorrow."

Our other line was still producing an occasional beaver but it was easy to see Dwight's hobby was now "Trapping Lynx Hollow Creek." The next day when I got home I found Dwight standing by our kitchen table showing my wife two big male mink stretched out on a newspaper—from Lynx Hollow. "No beaver today," he had the nerve to tell me.

"You know, Dwight," I said, "I've never caught a mink in a beaver set. And did you know today is January 15th, the last day of mink season?"

It was now time to market some pelts. We had twelve dry beaver skins and not too good a place to store them for any length of time. The coon skins we decided to keep for home use—tanned rugs or coon-skin caps, and also a pair of muskrats that were incidentally caught. They were worth little on the current market.

We were tempted to try a local fur buyer before mailing them out as I'd heard once from another trapper he paid a good price. The company where I used to sell all my furs—Sears—was to my regret not in the business anymore. We trappers have been at the mercy of the fur buyers since the very beginning, and when you're lucky enough to find one whom you're reasonably sure is giving you top price, you hate to see him go.

A trapper picks up a limited knowledge of furs, of course, but it's a specialized business, fur grading. It takes an expert to know furs. This leaves plenty of margin for fudging on the part of the buyer; I won't say cheating because it's still in the nature of the age-old practice of price haggling. But let's face it: the trapper is at an extreme disadvantage in this kind of haggling. He's still being taken to the cleaners at every turn.

Dwight and I made a date with the local fur buyer and brought our skins in to him on a tarp, unfolding it on his cement floor. His eyes lit up.

"You've handled beaver pelts before, I see," he said, and began sorting them out, then measuring them. He got out his pencil and pad and began to put down some figures. I glanced over his shoulder and saw him write the words, two small, etc. Well I didn't know what kind of a yardstick he was using, but I did know we didn't have any small beaver. The smallest beaver in that pile was a 48 inch medium skin. So when he handed over the grade sheet, Dwight and I reached down and began folding up the tarp. We couldn't sell at that price or that kind of rigged grade sheet.

"Well," the buyer said then, "that big one there, I could give you $18 if it didn't have that bite through it." He had offered $15.00.

"No hard feelings," I muttered. "We just think we want a little more for all the hard work we've put in." We carried our tarp out, put it in the car, and drove home.

Later I wrote a letter to another company and received some quotes that didn't sound so fantastically high as some of those we'd been getting via the mail box, so I bundled up our furs and sent

Dwight Stevens and Don Murphey, trapping partners 1960-61.

them off. We received a check for thirty dollars more than the local buyer had offered. The big skin with the bite brought $18. Did we get our money's worth? I really don't know.

A large part of Dwight's and my trap-line was on the land of a private timber company. We had no difficulty obtaining a permit for this. There was beaver damage on another farmer's land in addition to that at Lynx Hollow, and we trapped there for mutual benefit of the farmer and ourselves. At all other sets we made certain we were welcome before going in, and it's a practice I can recommend for all trappers.

Now that the season is over, I'm actually relieved. Yet, here's Dwight talking already of next year. He made a good buy on some used traps—eight no. 4 Victor doubles and eight dandy light jump traps.

"Well, now just a minute, Dwight," I say to him, "we're not dug out from that flood of the last ten days of this season. Remember there are still four traps down on the Willamette if the water'd only go down, and there's one up on…" But he isn't listening. He's staring into space and thinking about those eight beavers he caught for Ronald Durflinger—on his own. I know when beaver time comes again he'll be out there. I'll probably be with him.

Editor's Note: This article was written in 1961 describing a bit of the 1960-61 trapping season. Things haven't changed much have they? Don Murphey died in 2007 at age 85. He hadn't trapped in over 25 years, but he enjoyed trapping vicariously through his son, Wesley Murphey, who still carries on his dad's legacy. Dwight Stevens died in 1964.

Bill and Joy Carla Murphey with their coonskin caps at the Dexter home.
(1957)

Wesley Murphey with a stringer of Wickiup whitefish. 2002

Whitefish of Wickiup

Wesley Murphey

I felt the gentle take at the end of my sinking-tip fly line and instantly raised the rod firmly to set the hook. The fight was on as the fish pulled to my right and stayed deep in the Deschutes channel near Sheep Bridge Campground on Wickiup Reservoir. The fish turned and headed on a long run downstream. The tip of my fly rod bounced up and down a few feet above the water's surface as I gave line through my right brake hand. After the long run, I felt the vibration of the fish shaking its head trying to throw the hook. I knew then that I had another whitefish. Over the next two minutes I gradually gained back much of the line, but the fish stayed deep.

The people on the bank and in a couple boats not far away watched with curiosity, some of them probably a bit envious that the fish was on my line and not theirs. One guy on shore, who hadn't seen the earlier fish I'd played, yelled, "Is it a big brown?"

"I can't say for sure," I answered, "but it's probably *just* another whitefish."

"They fight that good?"

"You bet they do. Any whitefish over two pounds will fight all the way to the boat."

21

"How big do you think that one is?"

"Gotta be at least three pounds, maybe four."

Finally the guy shut up and just watched which was fine by me. I was afraid he was going to conduct a full interview, asking me what I hooked it on, how good eating they were, if I'd been fishing long, who's my mamma and who knows what else.

Half a minute after the guy quit talking the fish finally came up about twenty feet away from my boat and rolled on the surface of the water. It was definitely a whitefish, of around twenty inches. I pulled in strips of fly line fairly steadily now with my left hand. Took some line, gave some. Finally, in about a minute I brought the fish alongside my boat and netted it.

"Nice job," the guy on the bank said.

A hefty Wickiup whitefish.

After I removed the hook, I started to put the fish in my cooler, but eagle-eye on the bank said, "Would you mind holding it up?"

I held the fish up so its body hung down.

"Nice fish," he said, then he and one of the other fisherman on the bank began talking back and forth.

I opened the lid to my cooler and placed the fish in the ice. The water at the surface in the Sheep Bridge channel that day was pretty warm, around 70 degrees. Whitefish, unlike bass, don't do real well on a stringer, and even worse when the water is warm. They spend most of their lives in the deeper cold water. Leaving a dead fish on a stringer in warm water is a good way to ruin its meat.

I caught my first Wickiup whitefish back in early August of 1983. It was a low water year and the channel downstream from Sheep Bridge was already down to river level. In the crystal clear water I could see several whitefish suspended about a foot above bottom not more than fifteen feet away from shore. A quick flash of silver each time a fish moved to one side or the other told me they were feeding on various tiny food morsels drifting within their range. I knew they'd take a fly if I could find a way to get it down to them.

The water was much swifter than the casual observer would believe, making it next to impossible to get an un-weighted fly deep enough. It's frustrating when you can see nice-sized fish feeding and can't reach them with your fly. In this case it wasn't the distance away, but the depth that was screwing me up. I switched over to my spin-cast rod and reel, put on some weight, a bubble and a small nymph. In no time at all I was hooked into my first Wickiup whitefish and found just how good a fight they could put up in a strong current. It was the first of three or four I caught there in half an hour before having to quit in order to go break camp and, unfortunately, head back over the Willamette Pass to the Willamette Valley where I lived then.

I grew up catching whitefish on the Willamette River downstream of Dexter Dam from 8th grade through high school. My friends, Jay Lohner, Tim Mole, along with my twin brother, Rob, and I fished the Willamette many times during those years. Jay and I, however, were the two that couldn't get enough fishing in whether on the Willamette River, nearby Lost Creek, or some other body of water within bicycling (then later driving) distance, or someplace one or the other of our parents would shuttle us to.

On the Willamette, we caught far more whitefish than trout, which included rainbows and cutthroats. There was no limit on the whitefish bag. We mostly used spinning gear; a small-to medium-sized single-bladed Indiana spinner was a killer. It wasn't unusual

Whitefish can get pretty fat in Wickiup Reservoir.

The author's wife, Jill Murphey, with a nice whitefish. (2011)

for each of us to fill at least half of the canvas creel that we each packed. My creel was often loaded to the top with whitefish; in fact I had it so weighted down with them some times that I wore it out and had to buy a new creel. We caught most of our whitefish in the lower two-thirds of the long rolling pools. They typically ranged in size from eleven to sixteen inches, occasionally we'd get one up to eighteen inches. But one time I saw one in the shallow edge of a riffle that had to go nearly two feet. Unfortunately, I couldn't get it to hit.

The Willamette River whitefish were not as plump as most of those I catch in Wickiup. But the bigger Willamette whities still put up a great fight. The Wickiup whitefish are actually a mountain variety, more of a silver color than the more slender-bodied darker-colored fish typical of the Willamette River basin.

Back then, we fried the whitefish up in butter like trout, though we scaled them first. It wasn't until I started catching Wickiup whities that I tried smoking, baking, or deep frying in a batter rolled in cornflake crumbs. They are good any of these ways, but especially batter fried or smoked. In fact, a couple parties of fishermen I run into at Wickiup—who come from other parts of Oregon to deliberately fish for Wickiup's whitefish—actually bring a smoker with them and smoke their whitefish right in camp. I haven't tried canning them yet, but one of these days I'm going to.

If I'm going to smoke whitefish, I just gut and scale, then freeze them whole, minus the head. For eating any other way, I usually fillet them. The two fillets from one average whitefish (15 to 18 inches) provide enough meat for a meal for my wife and me, by the time we throw in French fries, and a salad or pickles.

The key to good table fare with a whitefish is how you care for it beginning immediately after you take it off the hook. A whitefish is much more perishable than a bass, catfish or crappie, or even a trout. If you horse it in, and don't wear it out, you can sometimes get away with putting it on a stringer and back into the water. But as soon as you observe that it has died, you need to get it out of the water and into a cooler of ice, as mentioned earlier. The flesh will get soft quickly if you don't keep it cool.

I don't horse in the whitefish that I catch on my fly rod because it is so much fun to play them out. Besides that, they have a somewhat fragile mouth that can be torn. If I try to force them too fast, I sometimes either break my line or lose the fish. I lose enough of them as it is.

One weekend, a couple of good fly fisherman about my age were camped near us at Sheep Bridge and enjoyed giving me a hard time about the whitefish I was catching. At one point one of them walked down the bank and held up the twenty-inch German brown trout he had just caught on a #14 bead-head hare's-ear fly.

"Here's a *real* fish!" he bragged.

I laughed as I fished from my ten-foot aluminum pram in the middle of the Sheep Bridge channel.

Besides catching a number of smaller trout, he and his brother each caught one or two browns a little over twenty inches each day they were there, and his brother caught a monster male that measured twenty-eight inches.

I was on shore nearby, during the late afternoon, when the brother hooked the big fish; I watched him play it. The monster fish seemed to fight more like a salmon and did more holding than moving in the strong current straight out from the Sheep Bridge boat landing. I don't remember how long the one brother had it on, but finally the other brother waded out a little ways, about thirty feet downstream from his brother who had been playing the big fish, and netted it. They measured it, kept it in the water, let me and a couple other people there see it up close, then after swishing it back and forth in the current to oxygenate its gills, released it. It swam back out into the deep water. They estimated it to be about ten pounds.

I said, "Now *that* was a real fish."

I don't mind that many people don't think whitefish are real game fish worth fishing for. In fact, some people I've shown my catch to, either didn't know what type of fish they were, or were surprised to learn whitefish are not trash fish. Those who scorn my deliberate efforts to catch the mountain whitefish can sit on the bank for hours, or troll all day and spend tons of money on fuel trolling around the lake trying to catch one big brown if they want to. My family and I eat the whitefish we catch. Most the time when fishing for them, I catch and keep more than enough to easily pay (in price of fish from a market) for the gas it takes to get to the lake. And I guarantee you I'm having more fun than those who aren't catching any fish or are catching very few.

I've caught many whitefish in Wickiup that went 17-20 inches, which easily weigh between 2 and 3 pounds or more. I've also caught plenty of them over 20 inches; the largest ones went 22 inches and weighed 4 pounds. Pound for pound, I'd put almost any whitefish I've caught over two pounds up against the same weight rainbow or brown trout for fighting ability. I wouldn't say the same for every fish under two pounds. Most Wickiup whitefish I catch go over two pounds. In fact, I've only caught a dozen or so there that were less than 14 inches. That is the reason I can't get excited over catching the "put and take" planted rainbows of some of the other Cascades lakes. For eating, to me, the planters are bland and far inferior to whitefish. On the other hand, I really like the taste of browns, brookies and native or holdover rainbows that I catch. The planted rainbows are fine, however, if they're smoked or heavily seasoned.

In addition to the entire Deschutes arm of Wickiup Reservoir— including the Brown's Creek arm—whitefish can also be found in great numbers, and fished successfully, in the large Davis Creek arm. I suspect they could also be found down near bottom in much of the deeper portions of the reservoir proper.

Most people fish for whitefish with spinning gear, using enough weight to get down near bottom. I use my fly rod when fishing whities regardless of whether I'm using flies or some kind of bait because it's more fun playing a fish on the long fly pole and I get to handle the line. A spin fisherman can add to his/her fun by using a light-action rod and setting the drag lighter.

Whitefish—which have pig-like snouts and very small mouths— will take a variety of baits, including part of a night crawler, grubs, grasshoppers, caddis larvae, salmon eggs and a huge assortment of bugs. Of course they take some baits better than others. I've never tried power-bait, cheese, corn, or marshmallows myself on them, so I can't say how they work. In spite of their small mouths, whitefish eat minnows—which is why little spinners, like the Indiana spinners we used when I was a kid, work on them. When using bait or flies, small single hooks, size 12 or 14 are best, though a larger hook like

A cooler full of cleaned Wickiup whitefish.

a size 10 makes it easier to hook the whitefish and keep them on. I normally use a 6 pound tippet on my fly rod when fishing bait in Wickiup because it won't break nearly as easy as 4 pound test leader. I catch a lot of fish that go over 3 pounds and really big fish are always a possibility.

One other thing I like about Wickiup's whities is that you don't have to get out early or stay late to catch them. In fact, it's been my experience in Wickiup that they often don't start biting until the sun hits the water, after 8 or 9 a.m., they hit most the day, and then not so good in the evening. Just the opposite of trout. So if you're also a trout fisherman, you can have the best of both worlds fishing trout *and* whitefish at Wickiup.

Keep in mind that from July 15th through the end of August it is illegal to use any kind of bait in the Deschutes arm of Wickiup upstream from the ODFW markers near the West South Twin boat ramp. This change was instituted around 2005 to cut down on the number of big browns that were being caught there later in the season.

Beginning the latter part of August, Kokanee salmon are all over in the Deschutes channel—many in their orange to red spawning colors making them easy to spot— and can be a lot of fun to catch on lures through the end of the month. When they're spawning, however, they're not very good for eating, so you should throw them back to allow them to pass on their genes. It's a good idea *not* to wear them out completely before landing them. From the last week of August through the first ten days or so of September it's a treat to watch hundreds (if not thousands) of Kokanee spawning in the Deschutes River at Sheep Bridge. Same thing on nearby Brown's Creek. White pelicans, bald eagles and ospreys feed opportunistically on the spawning salmon in the Deschutes channel which adds to the thrill of watching. I've taken several friends and relatives from out of town out there at that time to experience what we locals can so easily take for granted.

From September 1st to the end of the fishing season the Deschutes channel above the mentioned markers is closed to all fishing. The Davis arm, however, is open for bait fishing all season long. Be sure to check the regulations each year.

If you don't think you'd mind getting teased because you're wasting your time on whitefish instead of browns and rainbows, then you have what it takes to get hooked on one of the easiest-to-catch, possibly the most abundant good-sized, good-eating, and arguably the best *fighting fish,* pound-for-pound, in Wickiup. Don't let anybody tell you otherwise. If they do, hand them a piece of that smoked whitefish that Wesley Murphey gave you. Once they taste that, at least they'll stop ribbing you.

Remember

Karl Keen

Sometimes the old man will just sit there and stare,
Remembering the day that he fought the bear.

He remembers his fights with the Blackfoot and Sioux,
And all the good times he had at the big rendezvous.

He watches the fire as the embers burned,
Remembering the hard times and things he has learned.

He remembers way back to when he was young,
About the day he almost drowned in the cold beaver pond.

He remembers way back to his early life
Back to the days when he had a Blackfoot wife.

He remembers his wife with her mood so mild,
He lost her one day giving birth to their child.

He buried her that day in the sacred ground,
A place where the air is still and you don't hear a sound.

Antlers in the Alders

(An excerpt from chapter in
Blacktail Deer Hunting Adventures)

Wesley Murphey

Shortly before dawn on Saturday, October 28th, 1989, I hiked into "Scott's Canyon" in the upper end of Lynx Hollow southwest of Creswell, Oregon. My destination was clearcut B, where I had killed a four-point on the same date a year earlier. I made the same approach as I had on several other occasions, including the previous year. Earlier in the season I had seen does, fawns and a couple spikes in the unit but so far no branch-antlered bucks. I knew the rut was beginning soon because I had seen some freshly rubbed trees in the last week.

It was cool and mostly cloudy with intermittent fog as I glassed the unit across the draw while the sun sneaked over the horizon in the east. No deer were visible.

Sitting in the same spot where I shot the four-point from, I waited for the fog to clear, which it did in about twenty minutes. Around 8:30 I heard a vehicle drive along the gravel road over the

32

hill in the timber across the canyon beyond the clearcut. A few minutes later, three hunters came over the ridge 300 yards away from me in the upper right corner of the unit I was watching and glassed the upper portion. They couldn't see much of the area I was watching, nor could they see me hidden in the shade of some young Douglas firs.

After several minutes, two of the hunters returned to their concealed vehicle and waited for their comrade, who I could still see, to answer nature's call. Theirs was the first vehicle I had seen there in three years. I knew the road was there, but also knew it was gated. They obviously had a key.

When the third hunter disappeared over the ridge and I heard the vehicle drive away, I decided to work on around the hill I was on to the east, side-hill and gradually work my way down into the bottom near the creek. The deer had been browsing heavily in the brushy unit and had numerous trails along the benches and creases. Hunting slowly, it took me most of an hour to round the part of the mountain facing south. I had worked down to about 100 yards away from the very young alders lining the creek bottom separating the big timber across the way from the hill I was on. Left of the big timber there was an older reprod unit of eight-to ten-year-old firs on a steep hill.

At about 10 o'clock, I heard some noise like a walking deer in the timber across the way and below me. At once, I focused my attention there and spotted a very nice blacktail buck with a large, wide rack. Not taking the time to count points, I immediately raised my rifle to shoot. Unfortunately, the buck was stepping right out— nose to the ground and obviously in hot pursuit of a doe—and reached the cover of the alder-laden creek bottom in the second it took me to ready myself.

When he dropped down into the ravine and out of sight, I figured I could get a shot at him coming up out of the draw on my side, but I wasn't in the right position. I was at least forty-five feet above him, besides an overland distance of over sixty yards, with a knoll between me and where I guessed he would come up.

Hurriedly, I moved about twenty feet farther down the hill to the left and readied my sights for him. When he didn't appear in a few seconds, I wondered where he had gone. At that instant, I saw him out of the corner of my left eye going through the alder brush on my side of the creek, but farther downstream than I had anticipated. I swung my rifle a few inches to the left, and as soon as I had the very front of him centered in my crosshairs, I squeezed the trigger. He was gone in the trees!

At once, I ran a little farther down the hill, stopping on a rise that allowed me to see a fair chunk of ground across the adjoining spring that ran in from the big timber behind me to the left. When the buck did not show, I was somewhat concerned because he certainly could have slipped through into the timber at the junction without crossing into the clear ground I was watching. On the other hand, not seeing him could be a great sign.

I hurried down to his position at the moment of my shot. Searching hopefully, I found him lying dead in the alders with a hole through his neck. I could not believe my eyes! He was a beautiful full-pointed five by four, sporting nice eye guards to boot! During all my previous years of blacktail hunting, I had considered a five-point foot-hill blacktail almost a mythical creature. Two years in a row I had killed my buck on October 28th.

After gutting the big buck and getting him up hill to my truck which was over a mile away, I hurriedly drove home with him. On the drive home, I turned repeatedly to get a look at my trophy in the bed of my truck. Numerous times I also gave into my excitement and shouted, "Alright! Thank you God!" while pumping my fist in the air. Maybe you can relate.

Wes with his trophy five-point blacktail. (1989)

Rocked and Nearly Rolled

Wesley Murphey

With otter prices over a hundred dollars, I finally gave into the urge to run a six day otter line the first week of March 2004. Work and wrestling coaching obligations had prevented me from running a winter trap line near La Pine in Central Oregon where I had moved my family the previous fall. But the wrestling season was now over, and I was in-between jobs.

Without adequate time to scout fur near our new home, I opted to pull my wooden drift boat back over the Cascade Mountains and trap a familiar stretch of the Middle Fork of the Willamette River. While in the valley I stayed at my dad's place outside of Eugene, near Goshen. Other than my skinning knives, sharpening steel, and a fur comb, I left all my fur handling tools, fleshing beam and drying boards at home. While at Dad's I just skinned my catch and put the pelts in sealed plastic bags in his freezer.

When trapping by drift boat, I normally trap relatively short stretches of river—five or six miles at a time—which allows me more time to read sign, set traps and adequately cover the area of interest. When I've completed trapping one short run I set up another, and sometimes I run two lines simultaneously alternating days. For this present otter trap line, however, I chose to drift a long stretch beginning at Pengra Landing, about four miles downstream of Dexter Dam, on down to Day Island Park in Springfield, over 17 miles downriver. With prices downs for beaver fur and beaver castors and it being so late in the season when many beavers in the Willamette River weep castoreum heavily on their undersides and also fight more—both factors downgrading the value of their pelts—I did not deliberately set any beaver sets. Of course, some of the best otter sets are also good beaver and nutria sets, so I couldn't help but take some of those critters as well. Most of the sets I put in were in places I'd caught otters from in previous years.

The Willamette Valley weather was fantastic the six days I had traps out; daytime temperatures were in the high fifties and low sixties. With the dry weather and upstream reservoirs now on their late-winter through spring fill cycles, water flow and levels were fairly steady but low—too low in some places. The area just upriver from the Fall Creek-Willamette River confluence was just such a place.

Each winter that I run that stretch of river, I'm always a little nervous my first run through, which no doubt is partly because it was there that, as a thirteen year old in September of 1970, I was thrown into the river in a boating accident while fishing with my dad and his brother, my uncle Jim Murphey. (See chapter *Trapping Season 1994-95* in volume 1 for that story).

But besides that incident buried in my memory, the river above Fall Creek is wide and contains several channels, any of which might be blocked off with fallen trees, logs and other debris, or in low water, be too shallow to float through. There's almost always some remnant of a broken up boat somewhere along that stretch of river, or perhaps a little ways downstream, indicating that some boater wasn't very lucky.

Today was my second run through. On my previous run two days ago, when setting out my trap line, I chose to take the left most

On the Middle Fork of the Willamette River,
upstream from the Fall Creek confluence.

channel mainly because it has always provided access to some good backwaters on the south side of the river. Unfortunately, today the river was lower. I dropped anchor in the tail of the long pool just above a riffle where a long shallow bar ran *diagonally* from the left bank of the river to the right, a ticklish situation in shallow water. The current carries the boat diagonally across the riffle, at the same time the boat is dropping off to the side. In real shallow riffles, you pump your oars using short, shallow strokes to keep your boat slowed down so any rocks you hit you hit gently. Of course you don't want to hit rocks with any part of the boat other than the bottom. But today this riffle was too shallow and hazardous to float through at all.

After I dropped anchor, I pulled the oars into the ready position with the handles resting across my seat, I got out of the back of the boat, grabbed the anchor rope and put the anchor in the boat. Then I simply hung on to the right gunwale near the stern and slowly eased the boat down through the shallow riffle, avoiding rocks sticking above the water. About two thirds of the way through the riffle, things looked pretty good, so I decided to jump back in the boat and pump the oars quickly to keep it straight.

Unfortunately, just after I jumped in, the boat picked up speed and turned sideways before I could put the oars to work. A second later it slammed dead center against the one big rock that rose to the water's surface at the bottom of the riffle. I heard the wood crack and saw water coming in the bottom left side of the boat at once. Compounding the situation was the narrow deep channel with its left bank a mere fifteen feet away from the end of the shallow riffle.

When the boat hit the rock and water began coming in, I focused on that for a second too long; the strong current grabbed the wide part of my right oar, which immediately pulled that side of the boat over hard in the deep pool. I was immediately washed up against the left bank, taking water through the port-side hole where the hull and the bottom meet, and my right gunwale was almost touching the water on the right side because of the force tugging hard on the right oar and the starboard side of the boat.

Quickly I rotated the right oar, which relieved the drag and took a lot of pressure off the right side, allowing the boat to right itself some, though the heavy current still had me washed up against the left bank. Water was pouring in through the hole. I struggled to get the boat away from the left bank, then quickly rowed to the rocky bar downstream on the right side of the river. By the time I got the boat beached, it had over four inches of water in the bottom.

I got out, drug the boat up as far as I could on the rocks and unloaded the animals and my gear from the boat. Then using all my strength, I managed to turn the boat up on its port side and held it there to empty the water that hadn't already seeped back out of the hole. When the boat was drained, I set it back down and drug it farther up onto the rocky bar. I got down and examined the damage and confirmed that I was in a world of hurt—stranded on an island

in the middle of the Willamette River, close to the confluence of
Fall Creek… and I still had a minimum of three miles to go to the
nearest take out under Jasper Bridge, though my pickup and trailer
were parked at the end of my trap line at Day Island Park, in Springfield, 14 miles downriver.

I considered my options. There were none. I only had once choice.
Somehow I had to plug up the 4-inch hole—no easy task—and at
least drift down to the bar on the west side of the river under Jasper
Bridge. I could walk over the bridge to the pay phone at Jasper
Store and call Dad from there. I walked around the island gathering
up material to make a patch. I also checked my two traps on the
island; one had a beaver.

The material I put together included a few short beaver-peeled
alder sticks, bark, moss, grass and mud. Fortunately the hole was
directly beneath the three-quarter inch galvanized pipe that supports
the adjustable front seat running beam to beam. The pipe ran front-
to-back from frame to frame and gave me a good solid point to
brace a couple of my beaver sticks against.

Like a beaver patching its dam, I crammed a bunch of green
moss, grass and mud into and around the hole that involved the side
and bottom of the boat. I then placed the bark up against my soft
patch, and used the stout one-and-a-half-inch diameter beaver sticks,
in combination with the galvanized pipe above, to put tension on the
bark to hold it in place. I felt good about the patch even though I
knew it wasn't water tight.

With the repair completed, I sat on the left gunwale and breathed in
the fresh morning breeze carrying the scent from the budding
willows just downstream on the near bank. I gazed at the tall cottonwood trees across the channel. The river had changed drastically
since that day thirty-three and half years earlier. But I remembered it
vividly. My Uncle Jim was no longer with us, and little did I know
then that this would be the last trap line I'd run on the Willamette

River before Dad died. The animals I caught now would be the last of my catch Dad would ever see.

It was on the Middle and Coast forks of the Willamette River in the summer of '79, several weeks after I returned from my four year Navy hitch, that Dad taught me how to handle a drift boat.

Dad's last winter trapping was 1979-80, but he lived the trap line experience through me for the rest of his life. On one occasion when I'd gotten discouraged during the winter when running a full-time trap line while I was a full-time single parent of my two young children, he encouraged me, saying,

"Do you know how much grit it takes for a man to be out on that river alone, day after day, contending with the elements and the risks, catching the number of animals you catch?"

I never forgot those words, or many other encouraging words Dad spoke to me over the years. Thank you, Dad.

A pair of mallards gliding downstream above the middle of the river drew my mind back to the present. There was work to do, traps to check, and a lot of water to cover.

I drug the boat back into the river and observed a little water seeping in through my patch. I pushed down harder on one of the beaver sticks, but it was as good as it was going to get. I put the animals and gear back in the boat and headed downriver.

Water continued to slowly seep in through my jury-rigged patch, but it wasn't bad. It didn't take long to decide that my patch was good enough to go all the way to Springfield. Of course, in the slower water between riffles and rapids, I turned the boat around and rowed downstream to cover the miles quicker. Every half hour or so, I used my plastic lunch box to bail water.

By the end of the day, I decided that rather than try to permanently patch the boat during my short stay at Dad's, I'd get by with my temporary moss, grass, bark and beaver-stick patch, and would bail water frequently throughout the day on my remaining two trap checks.

I completed the week with no further incidents. On my final two runs, I let the boat down by hand *all-the-way* through the shallow diagonal riffle.

My catch for the six days was nothing to brag about: 6 otters, 8 beavers, 8 nutrias, 4 muskrats, 1 raccoon and 1mink. But, as always, the financial reward was tiny compared to the fun and satisfaction I gained from once again carrying on Dad's trapping legacy.

Wesley Murphey with a big Willamette River otter. 2004

Bill Murphey fishing on upper Fall Creek. (1963)

A Summer Day,
A Mountain Stream

Don Murphey

Ahead of us was a driftwood jungle. Paul Bunyan, it seemed, had been playing Pick-a-Stick in this canyon. But there was a creek there—so my son, Bill, insisted. And plenty of trout. All you had to do was hop across those logs, lie belly down on a blackened snag and lower a small trout fly through a hole.

He and two pals had proved this when they camped out in the area the week before.

Okay, the game wasn't new to me; my first trout had come from small creeks just like this one. There was that place where motorists paused along a hot and dusty gravel-surfaced Highway 58 back in the '30s. A rusty old pipe led from a shaded pool farther back. You could refresh yourself directly from its spout or use the tin can that always hung on an upturned twig nearby.

There was little reason for any of these travelers to go beyond the drinking spout, but if they had, and were just by chance carrying a fly rod, they'd have been pleasantly surprised.

First came the falls spilling all over a mossy rockway, then farther up—the wide, still pools. Gnarled cedar trunks and fern-covered hummocks were there for hiding behind. And your reward—if you were cautious enough—a velvety-skinned beauty of perhaps seven inches. One of many.

Later, after frying them crisp in an open pan, you could easily believe it was fresh smelt you'd captured after all.

Bill suddenly swung his line upward and had a trout dangling even before Wes and I reached the logs. Together we probed wood caverns and narrow slits between the logs, sometimes drawing our lines to within inches of the rod tip, dapping a shady pocket.

Wes and Bill Murphey on Lost Creek logjam. (1966)
The logjam washed out in heavy winter flood 1971-72.

If a trout was there the fly was struck immediately, though occasionally it had to sink past a log before being seen. Wes, younger of the brothers, bagged a six-incher after missing several strikes. At one place Bill squatted waiting, "Hey, Dad, this is reserved for you. There's a lunker in this hole!" And he was right, for after one cast I swung a trout of nine inches over my shoulder.

The log jams ended and tracing back the quarter-mile to the forks where we ate lunch, we decided to hike up the north branch. In 10 minutes we were enveloped by a dark canyon. The pools were deeper and the trout from them almost black, so little light penetrated their haunts.

Maiden-hair ferns on slender black stalks joined shade-loving rock plants to decorate the walls on either side of us. Ahead loomed boulders big as a shed.

Right then I couldn't help thinking how few people ever witness such unusual beauty, which for Lane County residents, at least, is so near at hand. The only footprints on a sandbar belonged to a traveling mink or raccoon.

This is upper Lost Creek some nine miles south and east of Dexter. But pull out a map of eastern Lane and take your pick of over a hundred creeks just like it. Though some are nearly dry in the lower reaches, there is usually water above with its complement of trout.

A few hints for the fisherman: Stealth is the by-word on the little creeks. Scare one trout and it's communicated to all others in the pool. The fly rod serves best with short accurate casts and dapping straight down the winning ticket. Fly patterns should be drab— black or brown on No. 10 or smaller. Flatten the barbs with pliers or knife blade so that small fish will be unharmed.

If you're a camera fan there will be plenty of seldom composed shots. Remember that light values are tricky in the dusky creek bottoms. Lens openings should be kept wide and shutters set slow.

We're going back up Lost Creek later but I'm not sure we'll take a fishing rod. For there will be a choice piece of driftwood to carry back and maybe a rock specimen or two. And, too, we don't want to be hampered when we climb over the falls. There at the base we found unmistakable evidence where men of an older civilization had cracked the shell of a creek boulder to fashion a crude stone blade.

The foot traffic up Lost Creek isn't heavy, true. But it's been going on—it appears—for a long, long time.

Billy Murphey, 8 years old, with fish from upper Lost Creek. (1959)

The Wrong Bear

Wesley Murphey

This story is a reminder that hunting adventures don't always go as planned and occasionally have not-so-happy endings.

After I finished my daybreak hunt for blacktail deer west of Lynx Hollow, south of Creswell, Oregon, on November 4th 1997, I slowly hunted my way back toward my truck on an old grown-over logging road that ran along a ridge through conifer timber with some oak and maple mixed in. Suddenly, I picked up a familiar stench riding on the breeze—a bear. I've always had a great nose and often smell deer or elk when hunting, and on occasion get the whiff of a black bear. I don't know how a bear smells to anyone else, but to my nose they are downright stinky.

Since I had my bear tag on me, I immediately checked the wind to determine where the odor had come from. Then I slowly continued up the trail in the direction of my truck half a mile away. The stink stayed with me and I became convinced that the bear couldn't be too far away and might even be headed in the same direction I was.

Suddenly, I spotted black movement off to my right. I stopped at once and released the safety on my bolt-action Savage 30.06 and slowly raised it to my shoulder. When the bear stepped out of the thick brush, I thought, "alright." But I had to wait to be sure there were no cubs. A second later I spotted the cub trailing the big bear. "Darn it," I thought, "so much for bear meat." I kept the rifle butt on my shoulder, but let the barrel down.

The bears continued walking leisurely straight ahead through small oak and fir trees for another twenty feet, then reached the skid road I was standing on only thirty feet away. The big, lead bear turned in my direction and headed straight toward me, though she hadn't noticed me yet. What do I do? I'd heard and read many tales of momma black bears attacking humans when they were too close to a cub. In a moment the mother bear would spot me, resulting in one of two reactions: either she would burst off to the side or she would charge. If she charged, I was already too close to get more than one quick shot off. At that instant, I reacted out of fear. I raised the barrel and shot the mom in the chest at a distance of twenty feet.

She broke away to my left and ran toward the edge of the ridge about forty-five yards away; the cub ran off to my right in the direction they had come from. I turned and got off two more shots between trees at the big bear just before it disappeared over the hill, then walked over to where the bear was when I shot her. Frothy red blood there told me that my first shot was fatal. Then I heard the cub cry off to my right, which made me sad. Yet at the same time I was excited knowing I was going to be eating bear meat soon.

I walked over to the edge of the ridge and saw more frothy blood, but as I looked downhill through the relatively sparse timber, I could not see the bear. The ground duff of moss, oak and maple leaves was scuffed up from the bear's running through. I decided to hike out to my truck and try to get some help from a friend to get the bear out whole. Upon reaching my truck I drove several miles to a house where someone was home and used their phone to try to get a hold of Mark Adkins. Mark didn't answer, so I left a message. It was now up to me to get the bear out on my own, since he wouldn't have any way to find me.

I drove back up, parked, then hiked back into where I had shot the bear. When I reached the edge of the ridge that the big bear had gone over, I heard the cub cry from somewhere down the hill below me.

A cub crying is a pathetic sound that I've heard on several occasions when hunting. One time while deer hunting up Lookout Point Reservoir, a bear cub ran across a trail in front of me and shinnied right up a tree to my eye level only fifteen feet away and looked directly at me. The brush around me was heavy, and I knew if momma bear came along about then she could pounce on me before I could ever get off a shot. I wasted no time getting the heck out of there.

Unfortunately, this time I had killed the crying cub's mom and felt pretty sad about it. I slowly worked my way down the hill following the path of scuffed earth with a little blood mixed in. There, about sixty yards below me, I spotted the big bear stretched out, belly down on the ground, facing away from me on a small flat. I hadn't heard the cub cry in a couple of minutes and assumed it had spotted me, hid and shut up. Then the big bear lifted its head up. I thought, "She already made my job much harder by going over the bank and down the hill well over a hundred yards. I'm not letting her go any farther." So I raised my rifle up, aimed at the back of her head and shot.

The cub rolled off of the big bear. *I shot the cub* in the head.

Sick inside, I worked my way down to the two black bears stretched out on the green mossy forest floor. The cub was lying on its back a few feet away from the mother bear. The sow had obviously been dead before I even left the area to get help, just as I knew she would be based on where I hit her and the frothy blood. The cub had been laying belly-down on its mom's upper back and neck, with its head on hers, but because it was identical in color and positioned perfectly in line with its mother, I mistook its head for the mother bear's. The situation that began as self-defense had turned into murder on my part, at least that's what I felt right then.

Animal rights activists and many other people who swallow the rightists' propaganda want to portray us hunters and trappers as cold-blooded killers who never feel regret over the wild animals' lives we take. They'd have every non-hunter, non-trapper believe we actually enjoy inflicting suffering on animals and get our willies by the act of killing. They are wrong. Oh, I'm sure there are some heartless hunters out there. But they are the exception. Myself, I never enjoy taking an animal's life, but I do appreciate the role God gave me—*man*—as steward over the *animal* kingdom. I also greatly appreciate and enjoy using the animals' meat, hide or fur. The truth is most animals that die at the hands of man by bullet or trap die a much more humane, swifter death than they do at nature's hands. Nature can be downright cruel.

Standing over the two dead bears, holding my rifle, I felt deep regret over how the whole scenario had played out. "If only… But it was self-defense," I told myself, "and then simply an honest mistake that any other hunter could have made in the same circumstances." Most of the times I've killed a big game animal, I was elated, not only because I was successful in my hunt, but because I knew I would get to enjoy the animal's meat.

As I looked at the dead sow, I reminded myself that I now had a good portion of the best wild game meat I've ever eaten—a Western Oregon fall black bear. But now I had to hide the dead cub. I picked up the cub by its ankles and was surprised how heavy it was—I guessed about fifty pounds. I carried it about forty yards away and laid it behind a big log. I then covered it with moss and maple leaves, feeling very remorseful.

I hated to waste the cub's meat. But as I saw it, I had no choice if I was going to get to eat the mother bear's meat and thereby make the best of a bad situation. Did I break the law? How does fear and

Wesley Murphey with the big sow bear. (1997)

self-defense figure into the law on such rare occasions? Would a game officer have understood the unfortunate circumstances that put me in this bind? The people I know of that reported mistakes they made, got cited for it. I wasn't about to take that chance.

I walked back over to the sow, pulled out my tag, validated it, then wrapped it around a front forearm with orange surveyor ribbon. This bear was too big for me to get out of the canyon in one piece by myself. Still feeling the weight of my circumstances, I mechanically field dressed the bear. Rather than doing it in the usual manner of completely skinning the rear half of the bear out so as to keep the hide in one piece, attached to the front half of the bear's body and head, I simply cut the hide in half just in front of the hind quarters. Under the circumstances, the last thing I was thinking about was saving the bear's hide for a rug or wall hanging. I then cut the bear's carcass in half.

I packed the front half of the bear out first, then returned for the back half. I then drove to my dad's place and told him of the unfortunate scenario that had unfolded. He assured me that, considering the situation, I did the right thing. He then took a couple pictures of me with the front portion of the bear.

Before butchering the bear, I weighed all the parts of what I had carried out of the woods and it came to 205 pounds. I estimated that the guts and other internal organs I left in the field weighed about thirty-five pounds, which meant the bear's live weight was 240 pounds. Not huge, but not small either, for a sow. I ended up with 85 pounds of boned out meat, with fat removed. The fat filled a 5 gallon bucket.

If you've never eaten Western Oregon fall black bear meat, you've missed out on the best that nature provides. If you do get the chance to eat bear meat, be sure it is fully cooked (attaining an internal temperature of 160 degrees, all the red is gone) because— like pork— it can carry trichinella larvae, which can cause trichinosis. According to *Taber's Cyclopedic Medical Dictionary*, smoking or pickling bear meat will not kill trichinella, if present.

All of the bear meat I've eaten came from berry-eating Cascades or Coastal fall black bears. I've heard that bears eating out of garbage cans or feeding on salmon or other animals are not very good eating. So you might keep that in mind if you decide to kill and eat that nuisance bear in your neighborhood. But then again, maybe you could fence him in and feed him donuts, fruit and vegetables for a few weeks to clean out his system before you shoot him.

Warning: Baiting bears is illegal in Oregon and many other states.

Shack

Karl Keen

The traps still hang on the old cabin wall,
The porch on the front is about ready to fall.

The cabin is looking like an old abandoned shack,
Is the trapper that lived here ever coming back.

Has he been killed by Indians, or drowned in a stream,
The old shack still holds all of his dreams.

Over in one corner sits a large pile of plews,
His gear is all packed for the big rendezvous.

He rode out of this shack over a month ago,
To pick up his traps before the big snow.

The ponds are froze over with a thick icy glaze,
His horses still stay in the valley and graze.

Ice now hangs from the roof of his shack,
This old mountain trapper will never come back.

Trapping Season 1996-97

Wesley Murphey

We've had a lot of rain so far this late-fall, rivers have been way high. I hope this isn't a sign of what I'm in for this winter. In mid-November much of western Oregon flooded as badly, or nearly as badly, as last February.

On November 18th I had to "rescue" Dad (75 years old) from his mobile home next to Sucker Creek—in the Seavey Loop Road area near Goshen. He called my house and said Sucker Creek was up to his front porch and running into his laundry room. I drove through several inches of creek water at the Sucker Creek Bridge on Seavey Loop Road. Many mobile homes in the trailer park there were completely surrounded by water two or three feet deep.

When I got into Mobilife Estates subdivision where Dad lives (and where I lived half a block west of him for 16 years), I parked my truck on Blossom Street over two hundred fifty yards away from Dad's place, waded from there (in my hip boots) to my old neighbor Chuck Gilham's place on Del Monte Avenue and borrowed his canoe. I paddled it down Del Monte to Dad's place in the northwest corner on Del Rio Street. The current on Del Rio Street flowed south to north like a river. I made it across the current diagonally into Dad's driveway on the first try. If I hadn't I would have been washed up against the debris-laden fence beyond his place.

Dad was very relieved when I showed up. The water at his front porch was well up my hip boots.

"When I heard the flood warnings over the radio and television and saw all the water," he said, "I used a ladder to climb up on my roof. I stayed there for a couple of hours before climbing down and calling you."

Fortunately Dad was wearing his hip waders, because there was no way we could paddle back upstream from his driveway to Del Monte Street. We carried the canoe over Dad's hedge and over his neighbor's hedge to the next neighbor's driveway, where we then got in the canoe. From there, we managed to cross the swollen, hard flowing stream at a downstream diagonal angle into Del Monte Street, which was out of the main current. We then paddled most the way up the street. What an experience. Dad then spent a couple nights with us until Sucker Creek receded.

From November 26 to December 2- I had traps set up the McKenzie Highway, mostly in the Rainbow area. About half the traps were beaver sets, but there wasn't much beaver activity there. I just wanted to get a jump on the beaver season, figuring the beaver there primed a bit earlier. I ended up catching 5 beavers, 5 muskrats, 2 raccoons and 1 nutria. Then, between family issues and high water, I didn't set anymore traps through December 15th.

From December 11th to the 13th I was in Portland with my six-year-old daughter, Tasha, for a second eye muscle surgery on both eyes at Casey Eye Institute. (The previous surgery was done in December 1994.) Hopefully this will be the last one and her eye muscles will be where they need to be to correct the problem. It broke my heart to see Tasha's bloodshot eyes once the eye covers were removed the day after the surgery.

My Sweetie Pie, Tasha Lyn, with a muskrat and her oversized glasses.
(November 30, 1996)

December 16, Mon- Rivers are high due to continued rains and water being dumped from reservoirs. I set Harrolds Dairy, Airport Ponds (directly across Dale Kuni Road to the west from Harrold's upper field) and Camas Swale near railroad tracks north of Creswell.

Dec 17, Tues- Caught 12 nutes and 1 XL beaver. I got the beaver in Camas Swale. Harrolds always appreciate my trapping because every animal (and its potential offspring) that I catch on their place or at the airport ponds is one less critter eating their summer corn crop.

Dec 19- Caught 2 beavers, 14 nutrias and 1 coon. One of the nutes was eaten up. When trapped animals are partially or completely eaten (except for some bones and tail) it is often the work of fox or raccoons, but sometimes it can be an otter, mink, stray dog or birds of prey.

Dec 21, Sat- 2 beavers, 10 nutes, 1 coon.

Dec 23- 2 beavers, 1 otter, 5 nutes, 2 coons, 1 muskrat.

Dec 26- Will it ever stop raining? Water is quite high. I got 1 beaver, 11 nutes, 2 otters, a coon and a possum. It's getting harder to cross waterways and reach traps. Another nute was eaten.

Dec 28, Sat- Got 4 beavers, an otter, 5 nutes, and another coon and 'possum.

Dec 30, Mon- 3 more beavers, 2 otters, 5 nutes, 2 coon, 1 opossum, 1 muskrat.

Jan 2, Thurs- Heavy rains last two days, very high water. I somehow managed to get to all my traps and pulled all, though a 280 conibear trap was missing at Harrolds. Whatever animal got in it—I suspect an otter—managed to break the blackberry vine it was secured to and probably went back in the water. I looked around, but the water is so high I will have to bring the pram down here later to search the water with my probing pipe.

Today's catch: 1 beaver, 2 more otters, 2 nutes, 1 coon. I've caught all 8 otters since Dec 23rd on Harrold's place. Considering the most otters I ever caught there in a season before was 2, that's impressive. I think the constant near flood-stage of the Willamette's Coast Fork River here has forced them off the river. Season totals to date: 21 beavers, 65 nutrias, 8 otters, 11 raccoons, 7 muskrats and 3 opossums.

Wes with furs ready for the mid-season sale, January 2, 1988.

Jan 7, Tue- I set 31 traps behind Brings Recycling, near 30th Avenue and the north end of Seavey Loop. Good Beaver sign. I startled a big otter from the bank in the south central pond. I salvaged a dead XL beaver from the north central pond that someone had shot in the last day or two.

I've only set Bring's area one other time in the past for several reasons, among them this area is a favorite place for environmental, counter-culture, hippie-type people to go for walks; it's also a popular meeting place for gays. People walk in here to fish, play at the river and recreate, which in the summer includes skinny dipping. In the fall and winter, duck hunters like to hunt down here. Another concern is that other trappers work it sometimes, normally not a threat to my traps, but they can trap animals before I get set here. The part adjoining Wildish Land is gated off to keep motor vehicle traffic out, though there aren't any No Trespassing signs.

But with the water on the rivers so high, I figured I might as well hit this place hard for several days, *hopefully without losing traps.* Miserable weather keeps the winter foot traffic down, though the gays still meet in the parking lot and some people still go for walks. Compared to private land or hidden places on the rivers, setting here is nerve-wracking, I'm often looking over my shoulder to make sure I'm not being watched or to slink down or hide if someone comes along. Today, I had to lay low a couple times due to people traffic. I was setting a conibear trap in a channel behind the parking area when a guy came back there to answer nature's call. I had to crouch in behind brush to avoid being seen. My relief came only after his did, when he left.

Jan 8, Wed- Caught 2 big beavers and 7 nutrias at Brings, added 16 sets, a dozen just back of the parking lot where the Willamette River has flooded into. It's obvious the nutria have already been trapped here. Curiously, when setting the new area where the river water is flooding, I saw several bare-foot human tracks in the mud. I can't imagine why anyone would be bare-footed in the middle of the winter in 40 degree water. But in the Bring counter-culture area, I guess anything is possible.

Jan 10, Fri- I got a late start and pulled into the Bring parking lot at 9:30 am. There were already a couple other vehicles parked there. When I walked past a pickup with its uncovered bed, I spotted two superblanket beavers lying in the bed. Panic Seized me. "This guy has stolen my beavers," I thought. Immediately I wrote down his license plate number and scanned the area for the intruder. Seeing no sign of him, I hustled down to my newest sets nearby. Each of the first three #330 conibears held blanket (XXL) and superblanket (XXXL) beavers. Normally I remake my sets immediately. This morning, however, I wanted to check all of my sets quickly and possibly catch the other guy in the act. So I left the beavers in the

A couple of typical beaver dams on small mountain creeks.

traps. The other nine new sets held three more adult beavers and three nutrias. I was pleased but still nervous.

I walked back out to the road and walked the quarter-mile to the pond where my farthest traps were set. There I met a tall, slender young man packing out a blanket beaver in his pack basket. I introduced myself, and found the young man to be very friendly. He said he had never trapped before this season, but had bought a beaver trapping video and some traps and lure with the intent of catching about 25 beavers to make a blanket and some extras to pay for the tanning. He had caught three beavers (including the two in the back of his truck) in the four sets he had set in the afternoon two days earlier. He had gone all the way to the back after finding a couple of my traps so his sets wouldn't interfere with mine.

I told him of my panic upon seeing his other two beavers and told him I had caught six beavers right out front. We walked back to where I had a #280 conibear trap stashed in the blackberries, and I showed him how to set it by hand without using the setting tongs. We shot the bull a bit longer, then parted. I didn't tell him about the otters I knew were working the ponds. Nor did I mention that I had recently written the book **Conibear Beaver Trapping in Open Water**. After he left, however, I wished I had told him that he ought to cover his animals and traps in the back of his vehicle. The first time he has some traps or animals stolen either from his truck or on the trapline, he'll figure it out.

I then checked the remainder of my traps and had 4 more beavers, 3 nutrias and 2 'possums. Still no otters! While checking my traps at the last pond, I saw two otters playing out in the water. I could almost hear them chuckle to each other, "In your face you dumb trapper." Honestly, I enjoyed watching them, but at the same time decided I would look the near side of the pond over for some good places to set.

After resetting all my traps and packing the animals to my pickup (which, of course, has a canopy on it), I returned to the last pond with a few traps. I climbed up on a high point overlooking the last pond and spotted an otter swimming around. "Huh?" I thought. Then I went down to look over a point on the near side of the pond for a good trail. Unfortunately, it was obvious humans frequented the point, and I wasn't willing to risk a set there.

I walked back around the pond to the far side where my traps were set on dry-land crossover trails, thinking to myself, "Could I possibly have the other otter I saw earlier?" Sure enough, there was a large freshly killed large female otter in my #220. The other 220 on that trail was still empty. Walking farther along, I came to the next trail. Bonanza! An XL female otter lay dead in my 220 conibear. I've caught an occasional nutria, and one time caught a beaver in a trap while I was checking traps in the same vicinity, but to get 2 otters this way really topped off my day.

Today's final tally: 10 beavers, 2 otters, 5 nutes and 2 possums.

Jan 13- Got 2 beavers, 6 nutes, 1 coon, 1 muskrat

Jan 15, Wed- I pulled all but 11 traps from Bring/Wildish area. Only had a raccoon and 2 nutes.

Jan 17, Fri- Set 35 traps on the Hendricks Bridge to Bellinger run on the McKenzie River. River just now down.

Jan 18, Sat- Pulled remaining 11 traps at Brings. Caught 1 beaver, 4 nutrias and 1 XL male otter.

Jan 20, Mon- On Mac River I caught 5 beavers, 1 coon, 1 nute.

Jan 22, Wed- Picked up 5 beavers, 4 nutes and 1 coon. One monster beaver weighed 65 pounds.

Jan 24, Fri- Had 5 beavers, 6 nutes and 2 coons. Pretty poor going here.

Wes with a big McKenzie River beaver. (1997)

Jan 26, Sun- Pulled McKenzie line after church. Only 5 more beavers and 1 otter.

Jan 27, Mon- I set several traps near Springfield Mill Race in 40th street area behind the Pacific Equestrian Center.

Jan 28, Tue- 1 beaver, 1 muskrat from Mill Race.

Jan 29, Wed- Set Willamette River: Beltline to Hileman Park

Jan 30- Ran river line, a very good day, finally. Caught 12 beavers, 6 nutes and 1 coon.

Jan 31, Fri- Rain. Checked and pulled Mill Race area traps: Had 5 nutes, 1 muskrat and 1 mink. Gary Thill (a University of Oregon graduate student and free-lance writer, who was a reporter for the

Bend Bulletin for five years before coming back to the UO for his graduate degree) went along with me today. He's writing a paper on my trapping for a graduate class; he got my contact information from the Oregon Trappers Association. I'll be taking him in my drift boat on the river line in near future. (Note added in 2013, Gary was editor of *Aquatics International* magazine from 2002 through 2012.)

Feb 1, Sat. Water way high due to lots of rain in past couple days/ nights. Water so high, that I left truck and trailer near front locked gate (I have a key for access), knowing I would have to row the boat up the slough downriver from Hileman Landing to get it to an alternate makeshift takeout point on the flooded gravel road between the front gate and the park. Little did I know then how tough my day would be and how close I would come to spending the night on an island in the river.

Due to the swollen river, I struggled to pull as many of my traps as I could, but was unable to get to 8 traps. But that wasn't the worst of it. When I went around the first corner in the left river channel (left as you float downstream) above Hileman Park I ran into a drift-boat trapper's nightmare. The channel was completely blocked off by four newly fallen (since last run) large cottonwood trees which fell from the left bank and completely blocked off the river channel. The heavy water had washed out their root systems. These kinds of logs are commonly called "strainers," by river boaters because they allow water to pass through, but can trap boats and their passengers.

What to do? No way could I row the boat back upstream against the heavy current and over a rapid to get to the main channel. Fortunately, there was a deep eddy at the far right side of the flooded channel that allowed me to get out of the main force of the river. There I tied my boat off to a couple limbs on the nearest fallen cottonwood tree, climbed onto the nearly two-foot-diameter horizontal tree, then used my bow saw to cut off enough limbs to fit my 16 foot drift boat through. The top of the log was about 6 inches above water. It was hazardous; I had to be careful not to slip off the log into the deep water with my hip boots on. I might have ended up hung up under the logs with my boots full.

After cutting the limbs flush with the trunk, I got back in the boat, transferred all my animals (8 big beavers, 8 nutrias, 3 otters and 1 muskrat) and all the traps I had pulled to the back of the boat. I then climbed back onto the cottonwood log and carefully pulled the boat up as high on the log as I could, tied it off tight on the near side to a limb. Got back in the boat and tied it off tight to a limb on the opposite side as well, while it teetered, hoping it wouldn't slip back down. Then I got in the boat and gingerly transferred each animal and trap to the front of the boat to rock it over the log, untied the ropes and let the boat slip forward over the log. It worked.

Once over the first log, I had to do the same thing with a second log that was just far enough away to make things difficult. I was one very relieved and tired trapper by the time I got through that log jam. The other two cottonwood trees were submerged beneath the trees I crossed over.

After I got through the log jam, I drifted past my normal take-out (which was almost completely underwater) to the aforementioned slough. Normally I could never have rowed the boat into the slough because it was landlocked a few feet higher and separated from the river with a spring running out to the river. But with the water so high, I had no problem getting in. I should mention that I caught all 3 of my otters in the beaver channel that runs from Eugene Sand and Gravel beaver ponds to the Willamette River, just upriver from the McKenzie River confluence. It was no easy job locating them with the water five feet higher than it was 2 days ago. I was a tired puppy by the time I got the boat loaded.

Totals to date: 77 beavers, 119 nutrias, 15 otters, 18 raccoons, 11 muskrats, 1 mink and 5 possums.

Feb 5, Wed- Started back below Beltline as the river has dropped a bit. When at Hileman in morning to drop off truck and trailer, I hiked the bank along the park and through blackberries on trail made earlier by duck hunters to check out the situation where the cottonwoods had previously blocked the entire channel. As I hoped, the river had washed out a new channel between the rootwads of all four downed trees and the near, left bank. So I was able to get the boat through that gap today, though I still had to take the boat up the lower slough below Hileman and load it on the gravel road to the Park, since the road to the landing is still flooded over.

I was able to reach the 8 traps from Saturday. They held 2 more otters, 1 beaver, 1 nutria, and 1 muskrat, all dead, of course. I got them skinned and on boards this evening to save them. Because the water is still too high, I'm lightly set right now.

Feb 6, Thurs- Ran line to get more traps going as river has dropped some more. Only had 1 beaver, 2 nutes and 1 coon today. Got through between fallen trees' rootwads and the bank again.

Feb 8, Sat- River Dropping. I hiked in and scouted the cottonwood log jam at Hileman in morning and saw there was no way I could get the boat through the rootwad gap now with the water down. That meant I couldn't take the left fork above Hileman at all. Fortunately I haven't reset any traps on that fork since the first log-jam day. I had to stay in the main channel of the Willamette River and take the first channel to left *below* Hileman Park, then row back upstream against the current, along the bank of slowest moving water. I loaded boat at Hileman landing this time.

Today's catch: 8 beavers, 1 otter, 8 nutes, and 5 raccoons. Three of the coons were at one stop. One had broken the wire and escaped with my foothold trap, but I tracked it down and shot it.

Feb 10, Mon- The river was down considerably. I caught 7 beavers, 3 otters, 2 coons and 4 nutrias. One of the beavers and 2 nutrias (all killed in conibear traps) were eaten, after being left high and dry with receding water. I had a #330 stolen.

With the river down so much, I had a bear of a time getting back up to Hileman Landing with the boat. In two places below Hileman, I had to unload all the animals in order to lighten its load, carry them up the bank to where the water was deeper at the tail end of the next pool, then use all my strength to drag the boat upstream over shallow riffles to deep enough water to row upstream. The trick was I had to use my anchor by hand to keep getting new bites in gaining ground going upstream. It wore me out. Good thing I'm only almost 40 years old and still in my prime. Ha.

Feb 12, Wed- Water lower still. Longest, most strenuos day of my trapping career. Pulled all traps on Beltline run. Normally pulling a line is much easier than setting it. But not today. Had to carry animals—12 beavers, 8 nutes and 1 coon— plus some traps to lighten the boat's load, even farther and drag boat upstream in even shallower conditions today to get back up to Hileman landing as there was no boating the left channel above the landing.

I got home at 2:30 pm. Then, since the fur sale at Albany is Saturday, I unloaded the animals, dried and brushed them out, then went right to work skinning, fleshing, stretching and boarding. I finished up and hit the shower at 2 a.m. I have fan and heater going on high in garage fur room.

Totals to date: 106 beavers, 142 nutes, 28 raccoons, 21 otters, 12 muskrats, 6 possums and 1 mink. Will be a nice showing for the sale.

Feb 13, Thurs- Got up at 7:30 and set the Clearwater to Island Park run on Willamette with 21 traps. Was just too tired to get a lot more done. I will be stretching the trap check requirement here. But I'm only using kill traps now.

Feb 14, Fri- By late evening, I had all my fur ready and graded/ lotted for the sale tomorrow, except for some of the latest animals, which I will finish getting off boards and brushed out early in morning.

Feb 15, Sat- Had an excellent fur sale. One of the few times in my life I felt like I was paid for my hard work as a trapper. I averaged over $38 on my beavers and the other stuff did well enough to make for a very good pay check. Gary Thill, the writer, went to the sale with me.

Feb 17, Mon- Took my son, Cody, and his friend Andrew on Clearwater to Island Park line today. Had 5 beavers and 5 nutes.

Feb 19, Wed- I set Jasper to Clearwater, then drifted through to Springfield and pulled the Clearwater to Island Park traps. Caught 10 beavers, 1 nutria and 2 muskrats. The muskrats (a male and female were both caught in the same (7 by 7 inch) 220 kill trap swimming into a den. A first for me. At least the pair will get to Muskrat Heaven together. Not much sign on Jasper to Clearwater run, will pull next time.

Feb 20, Thurs- Set Pengra to Jasper

Feb 21, Fri- I picked up the traps from Jasper to Clearwater. Only had 3 beavers and 1 otter. I hurt my back unloading cousin Rich's heavy Koffler aluminum boat under Jasper Bridge. With the water low and the bar under the bridge going out so gradual I had to push the boat off by hand, which normally wouldn't have been much problem. Unfortunately I damaged (bent) the back roller earlier in the season when winching the boat loaded with animals up the steep bank and onto the trailer at Hileman Park, with its primitive boat landing. Now the roller doesn't work, and I paid for it with significant lower-back spasms throughout the early part of the run. The muscles gradually calmed down some, but from past experience

Double muskrat catch. Wes and Tasha Murphey, both have birthdays next week, 40th and 7th, respectively. Tasha's better fitting glasses. (photo taken Feb. 19, 1997)

I know it won't take much twisting or exertion to cause them to flare up again.

Feb 22, Sat- Ran Pengra to Jasper. Gary Thill (the writer) went along today. Had 8 beavers, 2 otters and 3 nutes. I had to take pain pills for my back. Had a few sprung traps near new large log-cabin-style house next to left river channel half a mile above Jasper Park that I'm almost positive were sprung by the landowners across the slough and shallow channel. They saw me setting the traps, and they have a boat on the river bank that they could easily have used to get to my traps. They were outside today watching me work. The way the traps were sprung and not moved in shallow water, but with the support sticks missing, just doesn't happen on their own or by an animal.

Note added after season- Gary wrote a paper on his experiences with me—both times on the line and in my fur shed and also up at the Fur Sale last weekend. He's obviously a liberal (What else would you expect from a U of O graduate student? I know that's an unfair stereotype, but this is my journal so I'm allowed to express my thoughts.) and I wasn't thrilled with his write up, though I could see he at least tried to be objective. It's just hard for a liberal to not see things through liberal eyes.

If the liberals had their way, they would shut down all hunting, trapping and severely restrict gun ownership. That way the animals could be a huge nuisance to man and have massive die-offs from diseases that love over-crowded animal populations. Also criminals could commit their crimes without having to worry or consider the possibility that homeowners or private citizens might be armed, ready and able to defend themselves, their loved ones and their property.

Feb 24, Mon- Caught 8 more beavers, 2 nutes and a muskrat.

Feb 26, Wed- Pulled the traps to end my season. Caught 5 beavers and a mink. Will take this second batch of fur to Klamath Falls Fur Sale at end of March.

Many of these late-season beavers from the Willamette River have significant staining on their belly fur around the vent, back leg areas, and even up their tummy's from the castoreum weeping onto them when they rest or sleep with their tail tucked under them. The reason this is true of many of the late season beavers on the big western rivers is that mating season is in progress and the beavers' castor glands operate on supply and demand. In contrast to remote creeks that are normally made up of one beaver colony in which the beavers are related, the beavers on big waters are often unrelated and can be very territorial. Since they are marking their territory liberally with multiple castor mounds to say, "I'm available," or "This area and gal or guy is already taken, so bug off or else," their glands are often saturated in the late winter and spring with castoreum, which easily leaks out.

It's true that beavers are monogamous and normally mate for life. Unlike larger mammals and some other furbearers, beavers have strong family ties—the mating pair stay together full-time, often working side by side day after day, and sleep in the same den night after night. However, some beavers die each year (in traps or otherwise) leaving an adult single again. Plus a new crop of young beavers reaches sexual maturity and are investigating new territory and broadcasting their availability. And then of course, single beavers will sometimes try to take away another's mate.

I learned a trick years ago that has saved me from having many beavers drastically downgraded due to the orangish to black colored castor stains on the fur. When I skin the affected beavers out, I just cut completely around the edge of the stained fur and actually leave it on the carcass. I've never lost any size, by doing so because of the way I stretch my beavers outside the back leg holes. Before I started doing this in 1986 or so, I had a number of beavers downgraded sharply and called "Red Rims."

Final Season Totals: 145 beavers, 153 nutrias, 24 otters, 28 raccoons, 15 muskrats, 6 opossums and 2 mink. It was a grand season, in spite of some difficult water conditions. I made over $7,000, which represents a heck of a lot of hard work. But I got to be my own boss, enjoy the anticipation of checking each trap, connect with nature in a way few people ever get to, and keep an important part of America's and Oregon's Heritage alive. Oregon, the beaver state.

Wes and Jill Murphey with granddaughter, Brooklyn, at annual Oregon Trappers' Rendezvous, Waldo Lake. (August 2011)

Fooled by a Minnow

Don Murphey

In the best one-act play I ever put on, a fish played the leading role. It happened on the upper Willamette River, Oregon, the curtain rising on a June evening, just before dark.

Stage fixtures were: a rambling ripple of that perfect dry fly water that is two feet deep over river gravel, ten-thousand air-borne insects, and a steel railroad trestle.

The main audience was on the railroad trestle forty feet above and to my left—three fishermen who'd been working the far side of the river with bait. When the full force of the fly hatch arrived they'd given up.

To my right, higher on the riffle, was my partner, Tom Montgomery, then a high school student from Dexter, Oregon. The last words we'd exchanged before I'd drifted downstream pretty well catalogued the situation.

"Must be hundreds of whitefish out there," said Tom, giving a yank and quick haul-back simultaneously, and missing another silver and gray rise.

"Yeah, but do you see those pink flashes every so often? Some rainbow mixed in with 'em," I'd added.

One fish hooked out of five hits is a good average on rising whitefish. Near the trestle now it was about time to hook one as I'd missed at least four. My fly didn't want to float. Did it ever? As it pulled under half through a normal drift, I said impatiently, "Sink then- I'll help you!" and handed out several more feet of fly line.

A strike came someplace under the surface as the fly was making a half moon sweep, and it was a rod quaker. A moment later I heard one of the fellows on the trestle exclaim, "He's got a good one on now!"

Tom saw the bend of my rod even from a distance and shouted, "What is it?"

"It's no whitefish, brother!" I answered.

But the fish didn't jump— only stayed down deep, and soon I began to suspect it might not be a trout at all. Or a whitefish either. A reflection from its yellowish side then confirmed that suspicion. It didn't change anything, however. By this time I was in the thing up to my ears and committed to playing it to the hilt. Suddenly that fish and I were a team. I gave him every foot of line he could wriggle away with and I even helped him to splash the surface a couple of times, probably to his own astonishment. After we had worked under the trestle and some distance downstream I decided it was time to land him. He was virtually dead. No fish in the world ever put up such a valiant effort, for its size.

My audience on the trestle had lived every strain of my fly rod and they cheered with feeling as I worked the nearly dead fish to shore. I'd gambled that in the prevailing dusk at that distance they couldn't know what the fish really was, so I finished the play in grand style to clinch the act. Sliding my fish up on a sand bar, I pounced on it, held it at arm's length in the air for a very brief moment, then killed it and laid it gently in my creel, curling it around the front inside wicker wall. It would go about twenty inches.

The three men proceeded on up the tracks then, nodding and gesticulating. When they were gone from sight I flipped open the creel, jerked out the squawfish, and tossed it onto the bar for buzzard bait. Fooled by a squawfish! Ought to be getting used to it, I thought; so many times it has happened.

Here's a minnow, referring to that toothless family of fish called the cyprinids, with very un-minnow like habits. Most members of this family, like the carp for example, are bottom feeders. The squawfish, on the contrary, is a swift-swimming predator, a bully in whose company no smaller fish can feel secure. He takes a trout fly more readily than trout themselves do, much to some people's dismay. Yet, at the same time when it's necessary he'll scavenge, root in bottom mud or gravel, or do anything else that will help perpetuate his kind. When I say a squawfish will eat the same food of any other fresh water fish you can think of, including that fish himself, I know I'm on perfectly safe ground. I've caught them on most every kind of artificial lure that was ever tied to my line.

A study of squawfish conducted some years ago by fisheries men on the lower Columbia River resulted in a frustrating discovery, especially to those people whose job it is to hatch and release young salmon. These predaceous minnows had a habit of congregating at certain release points for the liberation of salmon fingerlings, particularly near hatcheries, and were consuming the baby game fish at a deplorable rate. One of the men in charge of the study, John R. Ulrich, Department of Interior, entitled a then current story in the Sunday Oregonian, *The Salmon's Deadliest Enemy*. This is all the reason any sport fisherman ought to need to catch every squawfish he can, but it's not the only reason.

The other reason may be learned on most of the larger, and many other smaller Pacific Coast streams. Like the one Richy Walker and I floated one June day.

Robin Murphey landing a squaw at our hole just east of Lowell Bridge.
Lookout Point Dam in background. (1970)

It was a typically gravelly stream, and a rain-drenched storm stricken one that day. Fly fishing had been good until the storm set in and we'd just changed to spinners. We came to a place where the river was cleaved by a gravel island and we landed the boat to fish from shore, each with a side branch of his own to cover.

I hadn't made but a cast or two when Richy called from the other side of the island, "Hey, want to see something?" He was pointing into a swift slick where the tail waters of a pool were squashed through a narrow rock gap.

The proud fisherman Robin Murphey. Who cares that it's a trash fish?

At first glance I remarked, "Suckers going upstream."

"Going no place you mean," Richy countered. "Those fish are holding in that current."

"You're right," I agreed, bending closer. "They *are* holding, and what's more they seem to be squawfish."

"Think they'll strike?"

"We can try," I answered, swinging the spinner out on my fly line.

The spinner wouldn't stay under; the water was just too swift for that. But it didn't have to. Three black shapes materialized behind it as it scratched a wake across the slick. As one of the shapes caught up to it, I yelled, "Yahoo! Out of the way!"

There was nothing but to follow the fish, out of the hole, through a hundred-foot riffle until reaching a lower pool where it could be played and landed. On my return trip Richy was already running the gauntlet, rock hopping to reach the low pool. Altogether we made twenty-four trips down the long riffle before the time factor of a float trip forced us to push off. We hated to leave that place; and because of the thrilling discovery of those squawfish that is one boat run I'll never forget.

The fish we caught that day were mature ones in the fourteen-to eighteen-inch bracket. Perhaps they were spawning. They were ripe fish in accentuated color, and they displayed the minute horny tubercles on the head that have some unknown connection to spawning.

Speaking of size, what little popular literature there is available on squawfish is likely to inform you that these minnows reach a length of five feet. As applied to the Columbia River or Sacramento Squawfish—two barely distinguishable species—this information is way off base and probably was intended to describe the huge minnow of the Colorado River which is called squawfish and is reputed to reach a weight of 80 lbs. Our fish will average a down-to-earth one and a half pounds with three pounders quite common. Five pounds is the largest I've caught or known to be caught.

A newspaper article with photo caught my interest once because it helped validate an opinion I've held for many years: that squawfish will, during the spawning run, swim up some of the swiftest, most unlikely currents. The photo showed the spout from one of those irrigation pipes emptying into a ditch. A number of fish had swum from some bigger water up the ditch and were leaping and making every attempt to swim up that irrigation pipe. I would bet that some of them made it.

As a high school youth, I—like the squawfish—had that penchant for getting into unlikely places. A lumber flume ran through our sawmill town of Dexter, Oregon crossing the main street at a height of about twenty feet. To reach the river a mile distant we boys would occasionally travel the catwalk rather than cut brush. If our nerve was up, and the mill was running, we'd hop aboard a rough sawn plank on its way to the planer and ride. So long as you didn't lose your footing, get caught in a jam, or meet the flume boss, it was clear sailing. That's one dare-devil stunt that will be denied my children—thank Heaven—because trucks took the place of the flumes.

Anyway, I'd never been to the end of the flume and suddenly one day I wanted to know what was there. It was Sunday and the mill was down so I trotted most of the way on the catwalk. Reaching the end, possibly a half-mile beyond the river, I came upon a beautiful scene. The flume that had been gradually dropping in altitude all along was built down abruptly allowing its stream to cascade into the lumber pond in a torrent. All around me were towering alders and ash, and I assembled my fly rod in perfect solitude. Many times we boys had seen fish swimming up the flume but they'd always gone too fast to identify. Now I would be able to tell them.

Fish were gathered in great numbers below the torrent, but they weren't the cutthroat trout I'd guessed them to be. I stood on a floating platform and caught squawfish on a fly until my arm was nearly finished. There were no trout there; there almost never are in a squawfish hole.

At the present time the Pacific states find a rough fish problem in the man-made reservoirs, particularly a squawfish problem. Formerly a river fish where natural forces helped keep him in check, the squaw finds the reservoirs too much to his liking to suit either sportsmen or fishery managers. One such reservoir is a few miles from my home. It is called Dexter Lake, and for many years I've driven along it several miles daily in my occupation as U.S. Mail Carrier.

At one place a side road intersects a main highway. You stop here waiting for an opening between heavy traffic of log trucks, freighters and cars; and sometimes it's a comparatively long wait. When I'm up against this kind of traffic I'll most always peek out of my car window and over the guard rails to see what's doing down on the lake. There's a little gravel hump down there, with a tree stump poking out of it, situated about forty feet from shore— a miniature island.

Around this island something interesting goes on. There are often good-sized fish churning things up down there. I can't say exactly how many times I had to see it before I was clambering around the rocky shore with a casting outfit. Not many.

It's one of the noisiest places I've ever fished. You listen to loaded log trucks grind to a stop, then shift through their gears, the very rocks you're standing on seeming to vibrate with every cylinder blast. Then pretty soon you don't hear the noise anymore; you can't be bothered with it because just off the island several small fish have broken water and are skittering hell-bent. There are five big squawfish tails in the air at one time and you're reminded of a school of striped bass you once saw acting in a similar manner. There is even a crazy sea gull hanging about who doesn't know or else doesn't care that the surf is a hundred miles away. He's doing something he simply can't help— wheeling and crying in excitement— as bait fish are driven top-side.

Out goes your lure and almost immediately it feels as if you've snagged a bag of coal. Squawfish strike that way. You fight the fish in as quickly as you can. Maybe lose it. Since it's only a trash fish you forget that it can put up a pretty stiff argument. But you do want to get your lure back out there while the fish are in. In a few minutes it's all over and you must wait for the squaws to regroup for another attack, and in about ten minutes it's on.

Well, I suppose that's the reason why when I'm heading up the lake for a "game" fish, I'll often say, "Shucks, a cast or two for squawfish won't hurt anything." And why I sometimes end up spending all my time right there.

Tasha Murphey at the Lowell Squawfish Derby July 2002.
The derby coincides annually with Lowell's Blackberry Jam Festival.

Wickiup Bullheads

Wesley Murphey

The sun was shining beautifully through the tops of the ponderosa pine trees on that warm late-August morning as we headed out from the cove at Wickiup Butte Campground in my 14 foot fiberglass powerboat in hopes of getting into some good fishing in the main lake. We hadn't gone seventy-five yards when we came upon a guy in a boat in the narrow channel with a fish on. I cut the engine at once so we could watch him land it. In short order he lifted a catfish out of the water.

It was true. *You could catch catfish there during the day.*

Two years earlier, upon learning I was moving my family to La Pine from the Willamette Valley, a good friend had said to me, "There's some good catfishing in the south end of Wickiup Reservoir. We were camped there one weekend, when we caught a real nice mess of them while fishing off the sandy beach just around the corner to the south of the Wickiup Butte boat ramp. It was right in the middle of the day. Everybody was getting them."

One gloomy, windy afternoon, late the next summer, 2004, me and a friend, along with my teen-age son, Cody, were driving along the

84

top of Wickiup Dam's southern-most section south of Wickiup Butte Campground that is now gated off, when we ran into an older guy wearing a dark camouflaged jacket and wide-brimmed hat looking through a long zoom lens on an expensive camera that was resting at eye-level on an extended tripod. We stopped and asked him what he was photographing. Turned out he was on contract, doing a study of the bald eagles and white pelicans at Wickiup Reservoir.

"You should have been here a couple weeks ago," he said, after telling us a little about his study. "When the lake dropped off it left thousands of catfish stranded in shallow water in those flats—the eagles slaughtered them. They flew off with many of the fish they caught, but fed on a lot of them right down there on the rocks. You can walk around down there right now and find dozens of catfish carcasses."

If memory serves me correctly, he said he had documented 70 nesting pairs of bald eagles around the reservoir. He'd been studying them for months.

When he told us about all the catfish he'd watched the eagles slay, I was a bit concerned that they might have really hurt the catfish population that I hoped to hit on in the not-too-distant future. The first summer in La Pine had been a busy one for a lot of reasons, so I hadn't taken the chance to fish the south end of the lake. I had focused all my attention in the Deschutes channel near Sheep Bridge Campground, mostly catching whitefish, though I also caught some rainbows and small brown trout in the upper end.

Just for the heck of it, after leaving the bird expert, the three of us drove a ways down the dam and parked, then hiked down the dam's short boulder face to the rocky beach he had indicated. Sure enough, numerous catfish remains lay strewn about—many with flesh completely gone leaving only the head and skeleton, others only partially eaten. I guess eagles aren't as conscientious as the American Indians were when harvesting fish or wild game. Maybe they were too caught up in the feeding frenzy described by the bird-

Bald eagle in ponderosa snag 150 feet above ground at Wickiup.

watcher to worry about wasting food. I'm sure the local raccoons, coyotes, mink and scavenger birds were grateful to cash in on the eagles' leftovers.

One day when I was fishing the Sheep Bridge channel several years ago I observed one of the resident bald eagles swoop down and grab a large whitefish from a shallow area a hundred yards away, then fly in my direction and land on the east shore, a few feet up the bank, just downstream from my anchored boat. No one else was around. Over the next ten or fifteen minutes the eagle pecked at its prize, tearing away chunks of flesh and eating them, seemingly unconcerned about my casting and drifting the fly line less than forty yards away. It was a beautiful thing to behold. As I pulled the

Bald Eagle up to the left of its huge nest that is over 100 feet above ground in a giant ponderosa pine tree at Wickiup.

anchor off the bottom allowing the boat to drift directly out from the big bird, where I let the weight settle back on bottom again, I wished I had my camera with me, like I often do. Still the eagle kept eating.

A little earlier that day, from its perch high on a ponderosa snag nearby, the eagle had watched me catch a whitefish on my fly rod. It may have even considered diving down to try to pick the fish from just under the surface as I played it closer to the boat. I've had that happen. Over at Davis Lake one time, a sea gull swooped down and

Wes with a chubby 11 inch brown bullhead at Wickiup. (2010)

took the white streamer fly I was trolling, thinking it was a minnow. That had to be quite a sight if anyone saw it—me holding my fly rod fighting a sea gull thirty feet above the water's surface as it tried to fly away. Fortunately, the gull figured out pretty quickly that my fly was not a real minnow and dropped it.

Soon the white-headed eagle had its fill and flew away, leaving the front half of the fish. Within two minutes a black turkey vulture with its ugly red head swooped down, landed next to the whitefish carcass and went right to work eating on it—seemingly unconcerned that I was anchored directly out from him, about fifty feet away. Obviously he had observed the eagle feeding safely in my presence. Ten minutes later the big homely bird flew away, and I could see there was nothing remaining but the fish's head and skeleton. The entire sequence would have made some excellent footage on a camcorder.

I've watched bald eagles and ospreys catch a number of good-sized trout and whitefish in the Deschutes channel and other parts of Wickiup and fly away with them, though sometimes with difficulty. However, one time an eagle caught such a big fish that the bird was unable to fly off the water with it, no matter how hard it tried. The giant bird flapped its mighty wings steadily, while the large fish flopped around in the hold of its talons. I wondered if the fish was going to pull the eagle under. Gradually the big bird floundered its way to the water's edge and, over a period of half an hour, fluttered and lunged its way twenty feet up the very steep bank on the west side of the channel with its trophy fish. Another eagle—undoubtedly the mate—flew in close a few times and screamed as if encouraging it's partner.

Some of the time I could clearly see the big fish lying dead on the pumice bank, while the eagle stood resting beside it or picked at it with its beak. At that distance, however, it was impossible to tell what kind of fish it was, though its size pretty well ruled out a whitefish. I estimated the fish had to be over two feet long.

One evening a couple weeks before seeing the guy in the boat land the catfish, I had caught a few 9 to 10 inch large-mouth bass off the bank there using a nightcrawler, but didn't catch any catfish. We had combined a late afternoon swim at that inlet's gorgeous sandy beach with some evening hotdogs and marsh mellows over a campfire, while wetting a couple of worms nearby.

After the guy in the boat put his catfish in a container, we hung out long enough to see him quickly catch another catfish. At that point, I said, "Forget fishing the main lake right now. Let's get us some cats!"

I immediately took the boat back into shore where we hustled up to our camp to tell the rest of the family, and my La Pine neighbor camped next to us, about the catfish. In no time we were strung out along the south channel's drop off on the west edge of the sandy beach, casting our nightcrawlers out into the channel not far from the guy in the boat. We all caught a number of brown bullheads—as did a few parties of fishermen on the same beach, just north of us in the direction of the boat ramp. The fish averaged 9 to 11 inches, with the largest going 12. They were a little on the thin side, though I'm not sure why.

Back at camp in the afternoon, I filleted-out a bunch of the catfish, then we rolled them in a batter and deep-fried them for dinner, along with some French fries. We left the cats that I hadn't filleted on ice in the cooler.

Late the next morning, I took the boat across the lake and quite a ways up the Deschutes arm, then doubled back and went way up the Davis arm. I did a little fishing there, but didn't catch anything. As luck had it, on the way back I ran out of gas only half a mile out into the main lake from the Davis arm. So I put the trolling motor to work, and was gliding along at a slow, but steady pace when the positive wire to the motor burned up, leaving me powerless in the middle of the lake, with only a flimsy canoe paddle. I sat on the bow of the boat with both bare feet dangling inches above the water paddling toward the dam. I was making amazing time.

Relying on my Navy submarine navigation experience, and using the tower on Wickiup Dam and a couple of surrounding mountain peaks for reference, I estimated that at my current rate of propulsion, plus strong wind and waves on my stern, I would arrive at our Wickiup Butte campsite by nine at night... in two days. Every time a boat came past within a couple hundred yards headed toward the dam, I waved the paddle in the air. Most seemed to ignore me, but finally a boater swung over to help. We tied a line from my boat's bow to his stern and he towed me over to camp.

The brown bullhead catfish of Wickiup can be caught with a nightcrawler or various other meat-type baits and sometimes even lures most anywhere in the southern flats from opening day of fishing season in late April clear through to the end of the season Oct 31[st.] You can catch them fishing from shore or from a boat. However, there are times when a boat is a big advantage and can be the difference between reaching the feeding fish and not reaching them. That was the case one early-September afternoon in 2006.

My step-son Andrew and I were slowly trolling nightcrawlers along behind my 10-foot aluminum pram in the same cove where

Is it a bird, is it a plane ...?   (Photo by Marie Peterson)

No. It's a big Wickiup beaver! (Photo by Marie Peterson)

we caught those first catfish a year earlier—though the water was considerably higher now—when suddenly Andrew's rod jerked down hard. Immediately, he yanked back firmly to set the hook. The fish put up a strong fight, but Andrew kept steady pressure on it with his ultra-light outfit and had it alongside in a minute or so. I dipped the net under the fat catfish and hauled it into the boat. He grabbed his line and lifted the stout fish up.

"Now that's a Pappa Pump," he declared, using the term we used for any big, fat fish we caught.

As a young teenager Andrew had named the pet bullfrog in his home aquarium Pappa Pump. He caught it from a pond near home in Springfield, Oregon and fed it so many bugs and worms, that it definitely looked like a hefty pappa pump— whatever that was.

I immediately dropped anchor, and we started catching one pappa pump catfish after another. Often they took our worms before they reached bottom. Over the next hour, we filled my cooler with the cats we caught in about a 40-yard area. Outside that area, we couldn't get a bite. Watching us from shore a hundred and fifty yards or so away, several people who weren't catching any fish tried to reach the hotspot by casting nightcrawlers with heavy sinkers, but couldn't. Andrew and I felt bad about that, but not *too* bad. In fact we chuckled every time one of their casts fell miserably short.

With the exception of one semi-pappa pump eleven-incher, all of the cats were between 12 and 15 inches. The 15 inchers went close to two pounds, all the rest were over a pound. And every one of them put up a wonderful struggle. I haven't gotten into a school with nothing but big cats anywhere in Wickiup since then.

Wes Murphey and Andrew Silvius with Wickiup
Pappa Pump catfish. (2006)

Even though I haven't found the exclusive big catfish school again, I have used that same technique a number of times to locate a feeding school of catfish. I row pretty slowly when pulling a worm. Beginning at the Wickup Butte boat ramp, we row around that cove area to the south dragging a night crawler a little ways off of bottom. Invariably when we find a feeding school of cats it will be in water at least ten or twelve feet deep, sometimes nearly twenty feet. We've also found them, by chance, when dragging a Thomas spoon or spinner along, which they hit with gusto.

I've located a school of feeding catfish about half the time I've searched for them in Wickiup.

One time, my friend Matt Bales and I located the school around 1:15 pm, about 200 yards south of the boat ramp and started catching one after the other. Some of them were too small to keep, so we threw those back. But we were putting a nice mess together in the cooler.

Unfortunately, I had to be home by 3:30 to babysit my grand-daughter so my daughter could get to her job at Ponderosa Pizza. It was terrible having to pull anchor at 2:30, while the cats were still biting, in order to row back to the landing, load the boat and make the twenty minute drive to be home on time. My daughter knew I was fishing, and when I pulled up at 3:45, she breathed a big sigh of relief. No man should have a time limit on his fishing trip. You never know when the fish will start biting, or when you'll get into a school of them.

I know there are probably plenty of times that catfish in a school aren't biting. One time a guy in a boat with a fish finder not far from me in the cove south of the Wickiup Butte boat ramp told me the catfish were all over his chart. He and I tried casting all around and worked our worms on bottom, off bottom, and what have you, and neither of us got a single bite.

Besides getting into catfish schools, a guy can sometimes catch the cats during the day or in the evening in the shallows not far from shore. The cats can be spread out over a large area at such times, but there are so many in Wickiup that if you work at it, you can catch a good mess of them. You usually get quite a mix of sizes ranging from about 6 inches up to 13 inches or better. I heard someone caught one 19 inches long, but 15 inches is where mine have topped out. As fat and feisty as cats can be, I'd love to catch a 19 incher.

I can't speak from personal experience, but I think when the lake drops down a guy could catch cats in the two adjoining ponds just over the dam from the west end of the four-mile road. I'm sure they must be in the Davis arm also, and even way up the Deschutes arm.

I think that the bald eagles, pelicans, ospreys, herons and cormorants preying on the Wickiup bullhead population do more good than harm. Catfish produce huge numbers of young and over-populate a small pond in a relatively short time, resulting in all the fish being stunted. Sure, Wickiup is definitely no small pond. But I'd rather have fewer nice fat catfish, than tons of skinny ones.

So birds, eat your fill and then some. That goes for you Largemouth bass and German Brown trout as well.

Wickiup Reservoir with Davis Mountain. (Photo by Marie Peterson)

Princess

Karl Keen

This raven haired beauty princess of the Sioux,
He had to have her this one thing he knew.

Her father was chief of the Lakota Sioux,
He traded her for five horses and a hundred beaver plews.

She was in love with this mountain man,
She always rode beside him lending a hand.

He dressed her in trinkets for the big rendezvous,
Paraded her around for all to view.

This little Indian princess whose skin was so tan,
She was the envy of every mountain man.

She was a beauty dressed in doe skins and beads,
She gladly attended to all of his needs.

They lived happily together until the beaver were gone,
Then the two of them quietly moved on.

Trapping
A Liberal Perspective

Gary Thill

"Oh, they're gonna love this if they're antis," Wes says to me as the boat nears the new, two-story log-style home and its sculpted lawn.

The owners are sitting out on the front patio sipping drinks. They look harmless enough, but Wes is suspicious of most people these days, always looking over his shoulder like an animal waiting for its predator to pounce. He was suspicious of me too at first, worried I was another anti, wanting to do an expose on the horrors of trapping, especially when I told him I was from the University of Oregon.

"You're not one of them liberals are you?" he'd asked me over the phone. "Out to make trappers look like murderers, or something?"

No, that wasn't the point, I assured him. I told him about my trapping grandpa, used his past to get me in, even though at the time, I wasn't even sure why I wanted in. I told him I respected what he did, even if I didn't completely understand it anymore. He was still suspicious but agreed to meet with me anyway.

"People tell me I was born 100 years too late," Wes tells me the first time we meet. "I just don't understand the direction of society anymore."

I'm standing in his garage, trying to get used to the overpowering smell of blood, flesh and musk. As he talks, Wes is stretching a beaver pelt over a board that's shaped like a stop sign. First, he nails the skin to the board. Then he runs a knife edge over it to remove any excess flesh. When it dries a few days later, it will be a perfect circle with only a small impression of the beaver's original shape still left. It takes Wes about 20 minutes to clean-skin a beaver and another 20 to nail it out.

If the people on the bank were "antis" they could use Wes's garage for an entire anti-fur campaign. Skins of beaver hang from the ceiling like racks of clothing. Fox, coon and nutria pelts are stacked against the wall like boards. A mink skin hangs from the horns of a five-point buck mounted on the wall. In one corner is a five-gallon bucket filled with discarded animal parts: ears, feet, bits of fat and flesh, which Wes keeps adding to as he works. A wire holds drying beaver castors, the animals' scent glands, which look like small brains, spongy and red with blood.

It's a lot like my grandpa's trapping shed. Shiny, well-oiled traps lined the walls. Vials of vile smelling baits and potions that tricked animals into his traps stocked the shelves. Blood, musk and death hung in the air like the carcasses dangling from their chains, their brown, shiny eyes still staring from their sockets. Had they known each other, my grandpa and Wes probably would have been fast friends, swapping trapping stories and slapping each other on the back. Me, I'm not sure. If it came to a fight out on the Willamette today, I wasn't sure whose side I'd be on: the people on the bank or the man in the boat.

But Wes is just paranoid, I tell myself. It's really no surprise these people are out today. The sun is shining warmly, glinting off the Willamette River, and there's only a hint of the morning fog still clinging to the distant hills. This is probably the kind of day they had in mind when they built their house here.

From a distance, Wes must look like any other 40-year-old. His blue eyes peer out from under a well-worn baseball cap that hides his thinning red hair. He wears jeans, mostly covered by rubber hip boots, and a camouflage jacket. They'd have to see his hands to suspect anything. A cut on his left hand oozes red. Both of his hands are chapped and red and scabbed. They're the hands of a man who uses them a lot, hands, I can't help but thinking, of a killer. But to the people on the bank, Wes and I are just two men out in a boat, maybe doing a little fishing.

To Wes, the people on the bank are the enemy, antis. The kind of people who want to outlaw his living, declare him an unnecessary and unfortunate anachronism. Not long ago, I was one of those people. In some ways, I still am. I spend my time indoors, mostly sitting. I work in the landscape of my mind, not nature. Even when I go outside, my feet stay on asphalt roads or cement sidewalks. Nature is here. I am there. The world of my grandpa, a world I once knew, is now only snatches of memories, yellowed photos and half-remembered stories. I don't have to think about killing, anymore. I traded that life for computers, carpeting, chairs and convenience. Lately, I've been wondering, at what price.

As we near the house, two dogs begin barking. I've already pulled the plastic over the catch as Wes instructed—six beavers, two nutrias, and two otters—so there's no chance the people can see their shiny wet fur glistening in the sun. But Wes is cautious. This is my second trip along with him on his trapline, but my first on his drift-boat line. It's been enlightening and somewhat nostalgic for me, though not necessarily in a positive way.

When he gets out of the boat to check the trap, the dogs' yelping turns into a volley of barking and the people continue to stare. I just sit in the boat, not really sure what to do. A few moments later, Wes comes back with a frown on his face. The trap's been sprung, he tells me. It could have been a muskrat, they're too small for the trap to catch them, but they can still set it off. But Wes has his own suspicions.

Those suspicions are confirmed when we get to the next trap, which is still within sight of the house. It's sprung too.

"These don't just get sprung like that," Wes says picking the trap up. "Look at that. Even the support sticks are gone. That was done by a human, definitely."

Wes figures the people watched him when he set the traps a couple days ago and sprung them when he left. He tells me he won't set traps along here anymore, even though he saw a lot of beaver sign. "This used to be a good beaver area just last year, before that new house went in." It's the same problem he's had on the McKenzie River lately—too many people, too many sprung traps.

Sometimes, it seems like the whole world is against him and his fellow trappers. It started early for Wes. Back in high school, he was nicknamed "beaver breath," because even then, he was known as a trapper. It didn't matter. There was something about working in nature that made up for it. He doesn't like killing, but animals that get caught in one of his traps die easier than most do in the wild. He's seen the way animals attack each other. Many of the beaver he catches have battle scars, bites from fights where losing often means death. He knows that nature would just as soon kill as create, cannot give without taking. These are things I once understood, knew in a way only people like Wes can. They are better for it, more real.

They are also more stigmatized for it. These days the only place trappers feel comfortable are places like the fur sale Wes takes me to—a trapper's version of a social.

This year's sale is at the old Albany Fairgrounds in a rundown exhibit building with paint-peeling walls and cement floors. Rows of long tables are piled high with the pelts of beaver, otter, nutria, red fox, gray fox, skunk, mink, bobcat, badgers, raccoon, coyote and just about any other critter that can be trapped legally. Prices are up this year. Beaver are going for an average of $38—a far better price than previous years. In 1990 prices dipped to $8. Wes will get $4,000-some dollars for his beaver pelts alone. There's an air of celebration in the musty old building. Trappers walk from table to table admiring each other's handiwork.

"You see that one right there? That's a marten."

Wes is pointing to a catlike creature on the table. It has small ears, short legs and reddish-brown fur. Small claws poke out from its front paws. They nearly cut me when I touch them.

"Why didn't he skin it?" I ask, staring at the animal. It's the only one I've seen at the fur sale that hasn't been stripped of its skin, or teeth, or glands.

"Aren't a lot of marten anywhere in the country. Figured he could make more money on it like this. A trophy."

The "he" Wes refers to is Carl Berg, a man about Wes's age who he introduced earlier as the "best beaver trapper in Oregon," high praise from Wes.

"That's about as beautiful as a wild animal gets," Wes says picking the marten up and cradling it in his hand. He holds it close to his face, turning it first one way, then the other. It is frozen in a position that makes it look like it's walking.

"Rod caught over sixty," says Carl Berg, who comes over from across the room when he sees Wes admiring his catch. Wes nods and puts the marten back in its place. Apparently, Rod [Harder] is someone who needs no more explanation.

"Yeah, Wayne Negus used to catch a lot, too," Wes answers back.

"He's not catching any, anymore," Carl says.

"You know that crazy old guy used to hang on all winter?" Carl continues, looking first at the marten, then Wes. "Story goes the last year he ever trapped, he got snowed in down by Paisley. Well, they got this search party together and they're all ready to go looking for him when the guy comes packing out. Then he just wipes his brow and says, 'I think I've had me enough marten trapping.'"

"To think of what they went through back then," Wes says, shaking his head.

Around mid-afternoon, the celebration lulls as trappers seat themselves in a circle and listen grimly to their lobbyist [Rod Harder] run down the list of bills and proposals threatening their way of life. There are about 30 just waiting to spring. One in particular is of concern because it's a backdoor policy that could bite them later.

"This is how Measure 18 started folks," the lobbyist warns the group. He's talking about an initiative Oregon voters passed over two years ago. It outlawed the use of dogs for bear and cougar hunting. Initiatives are what trappers fear most, especially since most people have so little understanding, or sympathy, for what they do or who they are. To most people these days, nature is more like a zoo—something to be seen but not touched—than a thing that's part of them. It's easy to vilify people like trappers, blame them for what we have lost.

But there are laws in place today to keep trappers in check. When Wes takes an otter, he marks it carefully down on a record card issued by the Oregon Department of Fish and Wildlife so that the State can keep track, know how it affects the otter population as a whole.

[*Wesley's note*- *By the end of the season, trappers must have each otter pelt tagged by the ODFW, and turn in its lower jaw, with gender and the location where the otter was caught recorded on a tag the trapper secures to the jaw. The jaw is used to determine the otter's age. The same tag requirement is enforced on each bobcat taken by trappers as well. The ODFW compiles yearly statistics from report cards that each trapper is required to turn in listing his/her total catch, broken down by species and counties.*]

Wes's body-grip traps kill the animal within moments. There are seasons in place. Licenses that must be bought. Classes that must be passed. Can we say the same? We rely on development for our convenience. We want nature equally convenient. We want to protect it, as long as it doesn't interfere. We want it left wild, unless it gets in the way. Then we put it in a box that offers easy access, surround it with the subdivisions, mini-malls and shopping centers that everyday are paving over more and more of our wilderness, without which no animal, including man, can survive.

As our wilderness gets swallowed up and more and more people stop living off the land, fewer and fewer people—people like trappers—understand this. The Eugene/Springfield-area trappers' association is the biggest in the state with a couple hundred members on the mailing list. But today at the fur sale in the old Albany Fairgrounds building, there are only about 30 or so showing their faces. Only four of them look like they're still in they're 20s.

[*Wesley's note*- *There were only about 30 at the trapper's meeting, but many more returned for the evening bid reading.*]

Between 1985 and 1995 (the latest year figures are available) the number of licensed trappers dropped nearly 70 percent from about 2,500 to just over 750, according to the Oregon Department of Fish and Wildlife. It likes to call trappers "fur takers," which is supposed to be less offensive than trapper.

[*Wesley's note*- *The ODFW calls them "fur takers" not to be less offensive, but rather because in Oregon fur takers include not just fur trappers, but also fur hunters. Some species like raccoon, bobcat, fox and coyote are hunted by some non-trappers, who— except coyote hunters—must buy a fur hunter license and also turn in a fur taker report card at the end of the season.*]

When my grandpa had a trap line, he was still just called a trapper. I considered him a monster. The matching gray Dickies shirt and pants he forever wore became for me the color of death. His hawkish nose hooked out from his face like a predator's waiting for the next kill. His bushy gray eyebrows slanted just enough to suggest a Vincent Price-like evil. His thick, rough fingers were strong enough to squeeze the life out of anything. I'd seen him do it. It wasn't until later, when grandpa was gone, that I began to appreciate his skill as a trapper. He could skin animals like they had zippers. He knew by tracks I couldn't even see, signs I couldn't spot, where an animal fed, or lived. He could look at scat and tell you what kind of animal left it and how long ago. He knew nature like no other person I've ever known.

I haven't been part of that life since my days back in South Dakota, where hunting and trapping were inter-twined with family and tradition. What I remember most is carrying the dead things—coon, fox, pheasant—feeling their limp, still-warm bodies in my hands. Pheasants were the worst. The shotgun knocked them out of the air but didn't quite kill them so I'd have to wring their feathery green necks as I carried them through corn-stubble fields, feeling their spasms and trying not to look scared. There are pictures of me holding these animals. I'm smiling, standing proudly with my dad, brothers and grandpa with whatever animal we happened to have killed that day. But I never liked killing.

As Wes's truck rumbles to a stop, on this my first time out with him—on his foot line—I can't help wondering what I'm doing out here with *another killer* so many years later. Wesley Murphey once caught 19 beavers in a single day and 173 in a season.

Now, here I was, clad in a pair of rubber hip-waders and a rain jacket, following him through the drizzle and I realize it's not just that I don't understand what he does. I fear it. But at the same time, I'm attracted to it the way a child is attracted to fire and I have to admit the man is attracted to killing.

We're just on the edge of a Springfield subdivision, not more than 10 minutes from his home. In the background I can hear pay-loaders digging up the earth somewhere nearby, and I can't imagine where a trapper could catch anything here. But then I see the river and I understand. Rivers. They're gold mines for trappers, even when surrounded by development. No matter what the animal, eventually they all come to the river. Like the James and those cold

Furs hanging in Wes's garage,
beavers nailed on both sides of boards on floor. 1997

pre-dawn mornings with my grandpa, walking with him to an animal that he'd caught. Wes, who's been trapping for about 20 years now, has his own rivers: the Willamette, the McKenzie and this stretch of water—the Mill Race.

The first trap is on the side of the bank a stone's throw away from the subdivision area we just left. The rain is coming harder now as Wes is standing over the trap. As he pulls the trap from the muddy water, I feel the fear of death rising in me again.

But when the trap emerges from the muddy river with an animal in its grasp, I am strangely relieved. There is no blood, no contortions of pain on the animal's whiskered face. It is simply frozen in a photograph of death. The animal has thick, bark-brown fur, a scaly rat's tail, small black eyes and huge, yellow front teeth. It's unlike anything I've ever seen in South Dakota, sort of a cross between a beaver and a muskrat.

"Nutria," Wes says to me over his shoulder, the smile gone from his face now. "Was hoping for a beaver."

He takes the animal out of the trap and dunks it in the river, rubbing his hands through its fur and then slicking it back down smooth. Then he hands the wet mass to me, motioning for me to hold it by its paw as he is. I am hesitant to be a part of this, carry a dead thing again after so many years. But I take it anyway. It's heavier than I expected and I must grasp its velvety paw tightly to keep hold. I feel the blood of my own hand pumping against the wet fur, my muscles strain against its mass.

It is only then, with the animal in my grasp and the river roaring through me, that I again appreciate the full weight of death.

(***This article***, written in 1997, was used with permission. Gary Thill was a reporter for five years with the Bend Bulletin, prior to going on my trapline. He later served as Editor for Aquatics International from 2002-2012.) Comments [*inside*] were added by Wesley Murphey for clarification.

You guys catching any fish?

Mule Deer That Got Away

Wesley Murphey

Early in the afternoon on opening day in Central Oregon's Paulina Unit, we hiked along the base of the rock cliff overlooking a huge reproduction unit of very young ponderosa pine trees below us to the north. The light drizzle dampened our hats and shoulders but not our spirits.

I was carrying my bolt-action 30.06, but I didn't have a deer tag. My wife, Lyn, who was carrying a 30-30, and my seventeen-year-old son, Cody, who had a shotgun loaded with 00 buckshot, both had Paulina Unit rifle tags.

A week and a half earlier I filled my archery deer tag with a muley fork horn that I arrowed at a distance of twenty feet from my tree-stand up a young ponderosa. This was only my second season hunting mule deer with a rifle. Unfortunately, I had to stay close to my visually impaired son in order to legally try to help him fill his deer tag.

For all of my adult life I've mostly hunted alone, which gives me the mobility and flexibility I desire. But in this season of 2005, I felt handicapped in several ways. Although Cody's eyesight limited our mobility and diminished our chances for success, it was important that he had a good hunting experience. Like most young hunters, Cody hoped to kill his own deer, but also understood that we were after meat and weren't going to hold out for him to get the perfect opportunity for a shot.

Hiking along the boulder strewn base of the rock bluff was a difficult task for Cody, and at times frustrating, so we moved pretty slowly. I couldn't imagine what it must be like to be him, to not have the freedom or ability to just take off to the woods, a lake or stream by myself to hunt, fish or trap, or to have to rely on other people to be my eyes, especially in a hunting situation like this one.

Cody loves the outdoors as much as I do, though he prefers the wide open space of the Oregon desert over the forest, I'm sure partly because in the desert he can wander around without worrying that he'll run his face into a dead tree branch. But much more because he has enough vision to enjoy the desert's spacious blue sky during the day and its bright moon at night. He hears things that most people never will and enjoys the aroma of sage brush in a way that I can only dream of. In the desert he feels closest to God.

Some day Cody will have perfect eyesight. It's easy to wonder what his first question will be when he stands before his creator and redeemer.

Myself, I'd probably ask, "Why did you do that to me, God, give me so little vision? Why couldn't I have normal eyesight so I could do everything in the outdoors independently, just like Dad did?"

But Cody isn't me. In Heaven he will only stand for half a second before falling to his knees and raising his hands to worship God who he will see perfectly. His eyes, that only saw things on Earth through the thickest darkest glass, will see clearly face to face. There will be no need to ask, "Why, God?" He will know then that his time on Earth was like one step in an endless desert compared to eternity with the desert's creator. His disability on Earth won't matter then.

As we worked along the rock face, I led the way, watching for deer ahead of us and in the flat a hundred yards below. Suddenly, way off in the distance across the long crease that separated the slope we were on from the slope below the mountain to the north, I spotted movement. Yes.

"Three big bucks headed our way!" I said softly. "They're way out there, about five hundred yards, but they're trotting directly at us."

I pointed the large-antlered bucks out to my wife, then said, "There's an excellent chance they're going to come right up on this flat below us, but we'll have to get up on these boulders to have a good shot."

I immediately climbed up on top of a large concave-topped boulder, while my wife debated doing the same. Cody waited where he was; there was no way he could do any shooting at that distance.

As I sat on the rock, I aimed my rifle in the deer's direction to get a better look at the antlers through my scope. I would wait until they were on the flat a hundred yards away. No point in taking a long front-on shot, when I was almost certain to get a broadside shot much closer, if I was patient.

When the deer were about 300 yards away and had just crossed the draw still coming right at us, suddenly there was a shot fired from somewhere on the edge of the rock bluff above and behind us. I flinched at the sound of the shot, while all three bucks wheeled around, crossed back over the ravine, then headed uphill along the opposite side of the draw. Instinctively, I started shooting as they ran uphill toward the big timber we had passed through half an hour earlier.

I got off four shots before the beautiful bucks disappeared in the big pines over four hundred yards away.

"That guy on the hill screwed us up," I said. "Since he only took one shot, it's obvious he saw me waiting for the deer and wasn't going to let me get a chip shot when they crossed the flat down here.

He's undoubtedly been sitting up there watching this unit and we messed up his plans."

"Did you hit any of the deer, Dad?"

"I doubt it, at that distance and the way they were moving out. But I'll have to go down there and track them up the hill to see if I find any blood."

I climbed off the boulder and then hiked down the slope and across the flat below, through the draw and all the way up into the timber. It was easy to follow the bucks' tracks, but I found no blood. With my bad habit of not leading the target, my bullets probably hit ten feet or more behind the running deer at that distance. I've never done any on-the-wing bird shooting, and I killed most of my black-tails at under a hundred yards when the deer were either standing or walking.

When I got back up to my hunting partners, I said, "Welcome to Central Oregon mule deer hunting. I've never had anyone do that to me when hunting blacktails. If that guy hadn't been up there, I'm sure we would have gotten at least one of those bucks and probably two."

Late afternoon, the next day, I got two shots at two more big bucks on the run through trees, and again failed to lead them or draw blood. I was quickly learning that in central Oregon, where there is a lot of pressure, you don't get many shots on standing big bucks. It makes sense when you realize that any large-antlered mule-deer buck has had to survive at least two or three hunting seasons to have a big rack.

A few days later, we hiked a five-mile loop on a closed road in the Spring Butte Travel Management Area and saw three wall-hanger bucks and several other deer. Unfortunately, the one big buck I could have easily killed got away because of my poor hearing. I was a few steps ahead of Cody and my wife, when all of a sudden, Cody grabbed me from behind, jabbed his finger to our left, and said softly but disgustedly, "There are deer right over there!"

Immediately I looked to my left and spotted a buck with a huge rack just as it turned and bounded into some lodgepole pines about seventy-five yards away. No chance for a shot.

"Man that was a big buck!" I said.

"You're deaf, Dad! You couldn't hear that?"

"I didn't hear a thing."

"They were moving right over there."

"Did you hear or see them, Lyn?" I asked.

"Yes," she said, "but I was waiting for you to notice them."

One evening, we took a stand in a blind I built a couple months before the rifle season about a mile off the Cabin Lake Road. The slightly elevated stand was next to an eight-foot-high rock bluff and overlooked several fairly well used trails that merged a mere twenty yards away. I set it up in hopes Cody could possibly shoot his own deer.

Before the season I had taken him out and experimented to see if he could, in fact, see a deer well enough to shoot it if it were close enough. I set a brown cardboard box about the size of a deer's body on the ground at various distances and in various lighting conditions to see if he could hit it with 00 buckshot. The light had to be right, but with practice he was able to see and hit the box with the shot shell out to twenty-five yards or so.

With the wind in our favor, under the shady canopy built out of dead branches and lodgepole bows, Cody on my left and Lyn on my right, I laid back on the ground to get a bit of rest. I said to my wife, "Whatever you do, do not pull the hammer back on that 30-30 unless you have your sights aimed at the kill zone on a buck. At this distance, a deer will hear it and look right at you."

About twenty minutes later, about an hour and a half before dark, I heard the 30-30's hammer click. Immediately, I opened my eyes and observed Lyn's full attention directed toward the trail in front of us. But she hadn't raised the rifle to her shoulder. I eased my head up just enough to see over the horizontal limbs making up the front of our stand. A doe was frozen, staring right at us, standing broadside twenty yards away. She had come in from the right on our blind side behind the bluff. Within five seconds, she bolted straight away from us.

I stood up and stepped out of the blind at once, while releasing my rifle's safety, to see if there were any other deer with the doe. Two branch-antlered bucks of at least three points ran away between the trees. I was upset at Lyn for not following my instructions, though I just said, "Two nice bucks just ran off. That's the reason I said not to pull your hammer back until your sights are on a buck."

I took responsibility for not showing her how to get the hammer cocked silently by squeezing the trigger, pulling the hammer back, then easing off the trigger.

The two bucks were undoubtedly following the doe and would have presented my wife and son with the same close-range profile the doe had. But blown opportunities make for great memories too.

Throughout that twelve-day season we got about five full days and a few evenings of hunting in. We saw a total of at least ten or twelve big bucks, but other than the first two days, we didn't get any shooting in. The two tags went unfilled.

A year later, Lyn's and my marriage went the way of the bucks that escaped. The big difference, however, was it wasn't missed shots that did the marriage in, but rather it was the numerous well-placed blasts at me by Lyn's mother and other relatives that finished off the marriage.

Hunting camp comfort.

Wes bow hunting for elk near West Fir, Oregon in the late-season. (1999)

Cody and Malisa Murphey at
Oregon Trappers Rendezvous, Waldo Lake. (2012)

But we do see Him who has been made for a little while lower than the angels, namely, Jesus, because of the suffering of death crowned with glory and honor, that by the grace of God, He might taste death for everyone.   Hebrews 2:9 (NASB)

Mark of the Rat

Don Murphey

Nobody asked me why—after all those years—I came back to the little house where a newlywed man and woman made their optimistic foray into adult married life. They also didn't ask: where's Marge? How come those boys are here with only their dad? In logging-sawmill country it wasn't healthy to ask nosy questions like that.

The truth was I, the dad, didn't know why the marriage failed. Maybe it was a reversal of the old saw: United we stand—Divided we fall... for it seemed more a case where "divided" was the only way to keep from falling. We split the kids and went diverse ways.

Wes and Robin, twins at eleven years, were happy to be back in the nursery home and among old friends. The twins were happy, that is, until the rats came. Not a whole lot of rats, just enough to ruin our equilibrium... just one family of rats—or perhaps part of a broken-up family, like us guys.

Ordinarily a rat sighting or a stray sign wouldn't bother me. Back in the days when my dad and stepmother owned the Dexter General Store, I—as a high school student—trapped the rats that infiltrated the feed-room. When a hole appeared I nailed a tin can lid over it and set my trap, covered with a scoop of chicken mash. Worked every time.

Now in our new home—the boys and I—things were different. I was already under extreme pressure by working at two jobs, so keeping house was extra, and so were the rats. Wes spotted one sitting on the toilet seat, and when he approached, the rat plopped into the toilet bowl and was gone. Both Rob and Wes were frightened after that, neither relishing using the toilet.

I'd plumbed and wired the house in earlier days, so the first thing I checked after learning the rats were coming in via the sewer system, was a clean-out plug about forty feet from the house. Sure enough, the plug was missing. I set in a new one. Step number one completed.

Next I looked into my collection of steel traps—relics from a time in my life when I followed the pioneer way; carefree days long finished. Piffle! The only traps were No. 4 double long springs-dandy for beavers and renegade coyotes but way big for rats. Still if I set the trigger lightly enough... covered it with rolled oats... about half a box...

Later that night came a shout from the boys' bedroom: "Dad, Dad, your trap snapped; we've got a rat!"

"We've got one alright," I announced after checking, "but he isn't caught—only this." I held up about two thirds of a rat's tail. "That's going to be one mad rat," I added.

Things quieted down, *rat-wise*, for about a week. Then, not too long after I arrived from the shingle mill—my night job—I was languid in that area just before sleep comes, nodding, when I sensed a presence on my pillow alongside my head. Immediately there was a stinging, painful bite on my left ear. "You dirty stinking devil!" I shouted, as a rat jumped from my bed covers. I leaped out to give chase but the culprit had disappeared.

I dabbed at the wound with Kleenex and applied a band-aid. Then a scratching noise in the living room drew me; the sound was coming from a cardboard box that contained our mis-matched socks. The rat's in there, I deduced; he's in there and—if I work it right—he's mine!

A plan wasn't long in coming. I located my old logger boots; the caulks were still sharp. Next, I grabbed a sheet of aluminum flashing, which I quickly clapped over the rat's box. Taking the whole to the back porch, I inverted the box and placed it on the floor. Then I trampled it thoroughly until it was practically flat. I dreaded the gory mess that would confront me when I separated the mashed cardboard and socks.

As I hesitated, a live and agile rat bounced out of the ruins and flitted behind a wood pile. Now only its head peered out, beady eyes glaring, nostrils twitching. A sudden kick at the wood and I had the animal pinned. Then, grasping a nearby axe, I swung it like a pendulum and on the second try sliced off the head of the rat.

Twenty years have passed since that incident. My twin boys are married now and gone from my household. I've remarried. The scar on my ear from the rat bite never fully healed. It would continually crust over and shed skin—with my help that is. I liked to peel it, especially when I'd get nervous. My wife, a former nurse, would admonish me, "Please, honey, don't pick your ear."

About three weeks ago I began noticing a tenderness around the afflicted ear—a redness extending to my head. I consulted my doctor, who referred me to a prominent surgeon. Suddenly I was the focus of an ecstatic bunch of medical people. Surgery followed—a surprisingly extensive incision tracing a path around the top contour of my ear cartilage and into the skin at the side of my skull. As the doctor put it, "Surgery is the only procedure we have for the treatment of a rat tail, complete with vertebrae, that is growing inside a man. This is a first."

Medical theories are beyond my realm; how and why that alien organism—a rat tail—got into me is something I hate to think about. My surgeon has a theory. He has asked me to sign a release of a paper to be submitted for publication in a well-known medical journal. The piece is tentatively entitled: "A mammal tail growing under the skin of a 68-year-old human male—a possible case of subconscious mimicry stemming from a traumatic experience with the same species of mammal."

I said, "Okay, that sounds like a good explanation; what I want to know is: will the thing grow back?"

I can't answer that," said the surgeon. "I can only assure you it wasn't cancer—that is in the usual sense—and we did get it all. Uh… for the future… the symptoms will probably be…"

"Yeah, I know; I picked dead skin off the horny end of a rat's tail for twenty years.

Wesley's note: I know you're asking, "What is a fiction story doing in a book of non-fiction?" Actually, the whole story is true except for the part about the tail growing in Dad's ear. As a matter of fact, this story is only a small glimpse into the problems we had with rats in our Dexter house. I trapped a number of them myself. That house was one of several houses built side by side in the 1940s along the slope on the main drag (Hwy 58 at that time) through Dexter. Dad bought two of the houses a few years after returning from World War II— he served as a medic on a bomber base in England.

Dad owned both houses from the late-forties until 1975. He sold them after I graduated from high school and went in the Navy. Except for the 8 years that we lived in our big house at Pleasant Hill from 1960-68, Dad lived in one or the other of his two Dexter houses for all those years, while renting out whichever one he wasn't living in at a given time. Beginning sometime in the 1960s, that row of houses was in-affectionately referred to as "Poverty Row." I have to admit, I was always embarrassed about living in either of those houses. But the memories… *and the rats.*

Dad's ear never completely healed after the rat bite. When it wasn't crusting over, it was discolored brown with a leathery texture, this until the day he died in 2007 at the age of 85— that's

37 years of picking his ear. It must have been a nerve or viral problem similar, on a smaller scale, to what happens to people bitten by a brown recluse spider or some other poisonous creature causing chronic problems at the injury site. He wrote this article in 1990.

Wesley Murphey's mother, Margaret "Peggy" (Uthoff) Murphey, collecting drift wood with daughter Becky at Wickiup. (circa 1964)

FUNNELING FUNDAMENTALS
FOR BLACKTAILS

Wesley Murphey

"Did you see any deer?" I asked, as I met one of my partners on the dirt road in western Oregon shortly before noon.

"Yeah," Jerry answered. "I scared a couple in that area over there when I was walking the road 40 minutes ago." He pointed to a timbered tract 100 yards to the east of us. "One of them was definitely a buck. I think it was just a spike. The other one was a doe. From what I could tell the deer never left the area."

My neighbor Jerry Easton hadn't hunted since he was in high school 20 years earlier. But three weeks before deer season he had read a copy of my book *Blacktail Deer Hunting Adventures,* which he had bought as a gift for his younger brother, Mark, who graduated from high school with me. He said my book had inspired him to try hunting again. He had already been out several times in the first week of the season.

When our other partner, Dan Morgan, joined us fifteen minutes later on this second Saturday of the 1994 deer season, we ate lunch and mapped out a plan.

On Tuesday, four days earlier, I had killed a three-point blacktail while I was crossing over a beaver dam on BLM land, hunting in the Fox Hollow area southwest of Eugene. I used my general tag for that buck, but still had my Camas Swale *one deer* tag to fill.

"Jerry, that area where you saw the deer is a good place to set up a drive. Why don't you walk this road (which switched back) down to where those two draws come together in a funnel and get yourself up on the bank in a good position to see any deer coming from the draw. Dan and I will go up the road and run the brush toward you."

After Jerry had enough time to get into position, Dan and I headed the short distance up the dirt road. I stopped on the near side of the first draw and whispered to Dan to go on up the road and drop off onto the steep finger running between the two ravines. When Dan reached his starting point and began his push, I followed suit.

I had taken but four steps downhill into a vine maple patch, when two deer exploded from 20 yards below me. Instantly I released my safety and raised my rifle hoping for a shot opportunity. The big fir trees and underbrush interfered with my view of the deer until they jumped the ravine and side-hilled the point 70 yards below Dan. At that point, I saw the front deer was legal, but its rack was not big. I didn't attempt a shot. The second deer was a doe.

"They're coming your way, Jerry," I yelled. "The deer in front is a forked horn!"

In a few moments the buck in the lead jumped off the bank across from Jerry. A second later Jerry's gun sounded off and the deer skidded to a stop. I climbed back up to the road above me and ran down to see the deer. When Jerry got to the deer ahead of me, I hollered, "What is it?"

To my surprise, he answered, "It's a 4-point!"

When I arrived, I saw the deer was an average size buck with a symmetrical, but unusually short rack with four short tines on each side. I congratulated Jerry on his good shot. His bullet hit the deer right behind the left ear. Dan reached us several minutes later and the work began, as we had well over a mile pack uphill to my pickup.

The buck Jerry tagged on this hunt was the reward for a deer drive conducted in a geographic funnel that limited the deer's escape route options.

Funnels are good bets for blacktail hunters because they concentrate deer movements to predictable, confined areas. These restricted travel zones can pay off for solo stand hunters or hunters working a drive toward hunters on stand. In either case, stand hunters must be positioned (preferably elevated) so they can easily observe any deer passing through the funnel.

What makes a good deer funnel? This can vary depending on whether you plan to hunt the funnel on a stand by yourself or take the team approach. The basic ingredients I look for in the one-man funnel are: small benches next to steep hillsides or cliffs; narrow swaths of big timber or hardwoods bordered by clearcuts, open fields, or bodies of water; canyons running together; small saddles running between ridges; and isolated areas that are not hunted by others. I look over topographic maps to find areas with some of these necessary characteristics. Then I go afield to analyze areas that look promising.

The potential funnel should be either a natural travel route between bedding and feeding areas, or it should be where several different trails converge to pass through a narrow plot. Keep in mind that mature blacktail bucks prefer to traverse secluded trails through brushy habitat to reach their morning beds or evening buffets. But these can be found in funnels as well.

The best time to hunt a funnel-stand alone is during the last hour of daylight and the first hour and a half after dawn. Also, whenever there is a change in the weather—particularly immediately after a storm—deer activity picks up and the funnel is a good bet. Finally, the odds are good for action in a funnel at various times of the day (especially the morning hours) during the rutting season when bucks are searching out hot does. The blacktail rut usually begins at the end of October or the first week in November.

The two best situations for team-working a funnel are along canyons and narrow tracts of timber bordered by young clearcuts or open fields. Deer like to bed down along the sides of canyons and in timbered areas adjoining clearcuts. In a drive, the hunters are forcing the deer movement rather than waiting for deer to do what they naturally do. The beauty of funneling deer by a drive is that this technique can be successful at any time of the day and in various weather. In fact, dry conditions are ideal for doing funnel-drives.

When team hunting a deer funnel, the number of hunters will determine which types of funnels can be driven and how many hunters will be on stands. More hunters take more coordinating, but they can also cover larger areas effectively. Many of the canyon funnels that I hunt are tailor-made for the three-man approach.

Ideally, a creek or draw with steep banks should be handled from both sides; a pair of hunters moves down the canyon toward a hunter or hunters on stand below them. Generally, the hunters pushing should not get down into the creek bottom, but instead, should maintain some elevation. If a hunter comes in below a bedded deer, the deer is probably going to stay bedded and let him pass, or it will sneak out above and avoid contact altogether. If however, danger approaches the deer from above and the deer can see a hunter across the way, it feels more threatened and is more likely to try to escape down the canyon where the trap waits.

The drivers will want to make plenty of disturbance: throwing sticks and rocks into possible hiding areas below and slightly ahead of them, snapping limbs, etc. I believe that in most cases, the hunters should not talk out loud while doing the drive. If, however, a legal animal is spotted and it is moving toward one of the other hunters, yelling an alert (or using an agreed upon signal on a predator call) can be helpful. When working a short stretch of canyon, often at least one of the drivers will get a chance to see deer that are jumped.

Stand hunters should get to their positions quietly and by a route that does not betray their presence to deer in the tract to be pushed, and they must not be upwind from the selected drive area.

Long canyons can be worked effectively in the same manner as short ones. This is true whether the valley is in the timber or in a clearcut. The hunters begin their push near the top and work a section that is only about 100 yards long. The stand hunter will be waiting at the end of that stretch. When the pushers reach him, they swap notes and then one of the hunters will hike around to get into position downstream for another 100-yard run. This may seem time-consuming, but it is well worth the effort. If too long a section of canyon is pushed, deer may slip out the side of the canyon above the hunter on stand.

Besides canyon funnel-drives, another ideal situation is the narrow-timber funnel-drive. Here, you have a line of big fir or hemlock trees 100 yards across and 400 yards long running down a slope. This timbered tract is surrounded by a clearcut 2 to 6 years old in which the deer have been feeding heavily.

Four to six hunters can effectively work this scenario which will be broken up into short drives of 100-150 yards beginning with the top section first. Two drivers push from the bottom of the section in a zig-zag pattern going towards the stand hunters waiting in the shade some 30 yards or so inside the timber at the top. If six hunters are involved, the remaining two hunters would take stands just out-side the timber to watch for deer escaping into the openings on the sides. When the top portion has been run, the hunters move down to where the drivers initiated their push and set up for the next section downhill.

Certainly, there are many other funneling possibilities than those I've described here, but these will get you started. Whether hunting blacktails by yourself or with others, find a funnel, practice these fundamentals and fill your tag.

Wesley Murphey with a dandy 4 by 4 blacktail deer that he killed hunting solo in a geographic funnel (1992)

Running Wild

Ross Turner

I like to roam high mountains with
their meadows and their lakes,
spur ridges and high saddles,
and many timbered brakes.

Though I enjoy all God's creatures,
the large ones and the small,
to my mind those noble elk
are the grandest of them all!

There's big lead cows with their cunning
ways and young calves so hard at play
developing their muscles, and
honing skills they'll need someday.

And big old bulls with massive horns
that reach well down their back,
coats that tend toward chestnut,
legs and cape a real light black.

Their strength is unbelievable,
as any hunter will attest,
seems elk can run forever
and seldom think of rest.

They'll charge through dense pole thickets,
cross rock slides and deep snow.
I don't think there's any place
that those big elk won't go!

When autumn's near and Jack Frost
leaves his mark upon their land,
those big herd bulls stretch out their necks
and give a call that sounds so grand!

It's a clear and haunting whistle that
builds in volume and in pitch,
then stops, and with a few loud grunts,
his bugle's over with.

It floats on thin air across the gulch,
rings and echoes through the trees.
It's a sound almost primeval,
but a sound that's sure to please.

It's just his way of telling other
bulls within his sound
that right now is **HIS** place in time,
and that right here is **HIS** ground!

Sometimes his bugle's answered
by one not far away.
Without a doubt it's certain a
battle will be fought that day.

Then he'll gather all the cows there
to form up his own elk band.
And to ensure his species
that old bull gives all he can.

But, once the rut is finished,
he'll join other bulls like him
to winter over in a sheltered place
till the springtime can begin.

Then he's back up in high country
midst the meadows and the lakes,
spur ridges and high saddles, and
those thickly timbered brakes.

If reincarnation were a real thing,
a bull elk's what I'd want to be,
and on a high and distant mountain,
a-running wild and roaming free!

(From Ross Turner's "**Reflections and Recollections
            of an Oregon Hunter**").

*Bill Murphey, 15-years old, with his first deer, a beautiful
4 by 4 blacktail. (1966).*

Trial Crossing

Don Murphey

Editor's note: this incident occurred in 1936, years before Dexter and Lookout Point Dams were built.

The osprey hovered effortlessly above the river, neck curved downward, eyes intent on something below. At the precise moment it plunged straight down striking the surface of the water in a shower of spray. Wings that had been folded tight against its body to cut wind resistance suddenly shot out wide and began to pump furiously. For what seemed like several minutes but was really only seconds, the great bird struggled to rise again. It lifted itself power-fully and headed upriver gaining speed and altitude steadily, water dribbling off for a ways. The fish that was gripped tightly in its gaff-like talons gave one feeble flip of its tail and stilled.

Wayne followed the bird's course until it was just a speck disappearing over the trees far away, then reluctantly summoned his thoughts back to the edge of the river where he had found a large boulder to sit on. He hadn't wanted to stop and rest. Not that he didn't need it; he needed it badly after pushing himself the whole afternoon from riffle to riffle, sliding over slippery gravel bottoms, detouring deep places by crashing through vine maple entanglements and nettle stands. And casting, always casting.

All afternoon he had succeeded in keeping the incident shoved back out of the way. But like a big lead sinker, it was still hanging to his heart. As long as he kept on fishing, kept on catching trout, he didn't have to face it.

He tossed his heavy string of trout into the water near his feet where they half-floated, bobbing gently. They were piled up on a hazel switch that had a nice crotch in the end, one that had purposely been cut long so he could pull the top far up under his belt. He wound in his fly line and collapsed his hollow-steel telescope rod, removing the reel and pushing it into a front pants pocket. Then he made a coil of the gut leader, leaving the fly attached, and folded it carefully between the felt pads of a leader box.

Wayne didn't often fish the north bank. It was a long way from home and it meant fighting heavy brush along a lot of blank water before you got to the good part. But it was worth the trouble. At least it had been today. On the north side was a branch that cut a path off across a great rolling gravel bar, then meandered along an old, vacated river bank to join the main stream far below. It was easier to fish than the bigger water of the main river and it teemed with trout. He'd made the trip especially to fish the branch.

Relaxing for the moment, Wayne reached a hand idly down into the water and turned over one of the two largest rainbows. Then he held it with thumb and finger over the gills, belly down, so in the clear shallows it looked alive. He moved his hand to and fro watching the undulations of the speckled olive-green back. It had been quite a surprise luring three rainbows from under that cut bank on the other side of the branch. He had hooked all three but lost one, which rather irked him at the time.

The best surprise, though, was the cutthroat. And to think he almost passed it up! In the lower portion of one pool a small fir had slipped into the water. The current was pretty slow there and it didn't look like a place for a trout. But just the same, he had let his fly drift beneath the tree. Deep under the fir tree is where the cutthroat had struck. Now, as Wayne removed the fish from the make-shift stringer, he guessed it would go a good fifteen inches. Not as flashy as the rainbows, it was still a trim, handsome trout. Except for a splash of carmine on the cheeks, there were just the black spots crowding each other on a pale-yellowish background.

Wayne brought out his pocket-knife, turned the fish over and slit its belly from vent to gills. Here he paused to admire the blood-colored twin throat-marking from which the trout got its name. He finished the cutthroat and then dressed all the rainbows. He didn't bother cleaning the chub he had saved for his cat. He replaced the fish on his stick, washed his hands free of slime and wiped them dry on his trousers. He then stood erect and gazed out over the expanse of the river. There was a reason why he'd stopped at this particular place. Now there was a decision to be made.

It was three miles home by way of Lowell Bridge to the east. Wayne didn't relish the thought of beating his way through black-berry cane thickets and nettle patches to reach the bridge. As the crow flies—which meant wading the river—it was just a mile home. To wade or not; that's what had to be decided.

The river was still up slightly from late spring rains. Exactly what that meant in terms of depth in the main channel, Wayne didn't know. The bottom was plainly visible all the way across, but clear water was deceiving. It was swift out there, inestimably swift. Whenever a riffle was wanting at the tail of a long pool you could figure on plenty of swift water. The river here, he judged, was a hundred fifty feet wide, most of it being easy wading. Only the main channel would be difficult, and it favored the far shore. But there was something else to reckon with.

When you waded the river you always considered the water below. Should you lose your footing and be swept downstream, you wanted a place you could swim out of. Wayne was an excellent swimmer and took that kind of happenstance in stride. The situation here, though, was a deadly one. There'd be no swimming if you slipped here for below was the drift. If you were swept into the drift you'd be sucked under and you'd never come up alive. No one could swim out of that.

Wayne looked downriver at the great bleached-out mass of jammed logs and trash. Ominous in a fascinating way now, the drift was a friendly place when you were fishing from its top. He knew it well. Right in front where the full force of the river smashed was an unusual trout hole. His dad had shown it to him, and very few fishermen knew about it. The river had built up a high, pointed bar there which tended to split the current. On each side, the water rushed with angry speed against, under, and to one edge of the drift. A part of this tremendous force was spent and curled into a back-wash which, by some freakish phenomenon, formed a relatively quiet pocket. It was a very small pocket, but if you watched closely you would see the foam subside every few seconds and a clear, green slick appear. That was the place to drop your fly.

The summer before was when Cousin Bob hooked the giant trout in the pocket, Wayne remembered. He'd gone fishing with Dad and Uncle Bud; they had parked him on the drift—to get rid of him more than anything, Wayne suspected. Later, when it came time to go home, Bob told about the big trout. It had swum under the logs taking his fly, he said. A gray hackle with a green tail, it was. Of course nobody believed him. Nobody ever believed Cousin Bob's fish stories. Besides, who ever heard of a gray hackle with a green tail?

The incident was forgotten until about two weeks later when Dad hooked and landed a huge rainbow from the drift pocket. It was nineteen and a half inches long. Afterwards Dad had asked Wayne to clean the catch, a chore that was always done with pleasure. Down on the bank of the little creek that ran through the home place is where the fish were always taken, and Wayne had gutted the big trout first. He remembered that distinctly. Suddenly there was the gray hackle, green tail and all—there couldn't have been two of them. Bob had been telling the truth all along. These things flashed through Wayne's mind—a brief, single picture—as he regarded the drift.

It was time to get started. He would wade out to the edge of the channel, then if it looked too bad he'd return and take to the bank. Unless you got out there you couldn't tell, really, how swift or deep it was. If the river was wadable here he'd be home in no time at all.

Shadows were lengthening along the banks when Wayne moved out into the current. A warm breeze ruffled the leaves of the giant cottonwoods upriver. A blue heron sailed down, wheeled sharply, and settled into a knee-deep shoal up at Howard's Slough. A crane fly hatch was coming on and swallows were now descending for a last meal. In the slick run that preceded the rush into the log drift, whitefish began to rise. Below was the crashing impact of the frustrated river, foaming white and roaring.

Wayne edged outward moving crab-like and cautiously. The gravel in close was slippery with algae. Out in the middle the bottom would be hard and clean—a small point in his favor. He had already picked out a marker on the far shore, a gravel spur below which he couldn't afford to come out for that's where the water turned dark and deep. In his one hand he carried his collapsed fishing rod, a mere three foot stick, while the other was extended almost straight out for balance. Under his belt was the hazel-wood stringer of trout, the tails of which were now dragging the water's surface.

They made a nice collection, those trout. What a pity there would be no one to admire them. That thought alone was enough to take away any satisfaction he might have felt, to cancel any thrill that had occurred earlier. Not that he minded giving the fish to the Andersons; he often did so. Of course they never saw the trout as a particularly fine catch, only as so much meat. It must be like that when you're poor he'd often thought. Funny, out of all those kids not one knew anything about fishing. To the Anderson kids, being the best fisherman around, even better than most men, didn't mean a thing. The thought never occurred to them. No, he didn't mind giving the trout away; it was just that this time there wouldn't be the chance to show them off first. And that was important, almost as important as the actual catching. But he couldn't bring the fish home. Last night had decided that.

A wave of depression came over Wayne as his thoughts led him irresistibly back to the previous night. He'd first noticed the tension in the air at supper. Just before, when he came in from the barn with the milk, he saw that his trout were lying in the sink exactly as he'd left them earlier. And nothing was said about them. It was true Dad seemed to be taking less and less interest in his, Wayne's exploits, especially his fishing exploits. But it had always been a kind of ritual with Dad and him—Dad's fondling the largest trout, and then the hashing over of the day's highlights, the understanding nods and grunts as Wayne went into detail. That in itself wasn't so disconcerting—Dad was often very tired—but the meal had been too quiet. Oh, sis had babbled on and Mom had said a thing or two, but Dad had remained silent even after eating, which was unusual.

After supper when they'd gone into the living room Wayne had felt unexplainably ill at ease as he ventured, "Notice the trout, Dad?"

His dad didn't answer immediately. He picked up the paper and settled into his rocker with his pipe, then just: "I saw them." That was all.

Wayne, feeling crushed, was about to press it further when his dad started in, "Wayne, I think I've told you more than once you're a good fisherman- for a boy. I'm sure all your friends have told you the same thing. Frankly, I'm disappointed that being on the river apparently means nothing more to you than proving that fact—and proving it daily."

Hurt at first, Wayne was suddenly angry. "What's wrong with being a good fisherman; what's wrong with proving it? You taught me, didn't you?" he said, defensively.

"Yes, I taught you, but I also taught you there's more to fishing than catching fish- or I thought I had anyway."

"But the fish aren't being wasted, Dad. We're eating them; so are the people I give them to."

"Look, son," his dad had then said in a gentler tone, "give yourself a rest from the fishing, eh? Give the river a rest, too; she needs it on occasion."

"I can't see why," Wayne had counted then, "I do my chores—"

"All right," his dad cut in, "I'm not getting the point across." A pause followed as if he wanted to spare Wayne, then, "You're fishing alone a lot lately, I notice."

The words had cut deep and the argument was finished. Wayne had then walked out onto the porch.

Mom and Sis had stayed in the kitchen through it all, quietly doing up the dishes. Mom washed the trout and sprinkled them with salt and placed them in the cooler in a pan covered with a cloth. She would try to smooth things over between him and Dad—Wayne remembered thinking as he'd sat alone on the porch. But it wouldn't be smoothed out. It couldn't possibly be.

He had stayed there on the porch looking up at the stars for a long time, until it got real chilly, until long after the folks blew out the lamp. He thought about the river. Dad had talked—well respectfully, about the river—like it was a person or something; but it wasn't true. The river wasn't alive; it didn't talk or breathe. Why should you want to rest it?

It was true that he was fishing alone a lot, though. That part hurt. Even his best friends never fished with him anymore. They always gave excuses. But that was just envy because he always out-fished them, pure envy. Alone or not, he would fish again tomorrow!

The depressing incident all at once dimmed as the river's pressure forced Wayne's thoughts back into focus. His total concentration was now demanded.

It always paid to start high on the bar you were wading, and Wayne had done that, for he knew that with each step you lost ground. His muscles tensed as he approached the main force of the river. The current tugged strongly at his pant legs, flapping them. He stiffened his right leg- his downstream, anchor leg. His left remained bent and probing, ankle turned in, and foot groping for the hold that would permit moving the anchor another step. It was slow work. The water was much swifter than he'd guessed, though shallower. His hips were now under, but he realized with satisfaction that it would get no deeper if he maintained his present course. He forged ahead, step by practiced step, angling downstream, bending the river's power to his own advantage when he could.

Soon there was just thirty or so feet of channel to wade; but it was getting harder to extend his left foot. He leaned forcefully against the current. Once, twice, he tried to get a new hold, but both times the foot washed back and the lower, anchor foot gave way, slipping out of its crevice to become lodged against a rock below. It *had* gotten swifter, and deeper—he couldn't remember just when.

He tried jumping ahead, lifting his right foot from its place of rest, taking a slight risk in the doing; but it was no use, and this time he was pressed back several feet before his anchor foot would lodge. Doubts now began to flare up and for the first time Wayne wondered if he would be able to make it. He twisted his head around and looked back the way he'd traveled. What he saw shocked him. He'd angled down farther than he'd realized. It was too far back! There was just not enough margin between himself and the drift to compensate for a return trip. It had turned into a one-way trip forward, and the impact of this knowledge left him sick and lonely inside. He shouldn't have been so sure, he told himself, so cock sure.

Wayne tried to fight off his uneasiness. It wasn't far to go, not nearly as far as going back. He mustn't get panicky, but he couldn't maintain this stance indefinitely. The river—now his deadly enemy—was pushing, pushing and something had to be done. His knees, weak with anxiety, now started to shake in unison with his flapping clothes. He needed time to think, but there was no time. Then, as if everything was all at once against him, he felt his toe-hold being taken mercilessly from him.

It started as a faint grinding sensation under his right foot that he recognized at once. Next it was a powerful heaving as the current forced a route under the boulder he was braced against. Then the river had it; Wayne felt the vibrations as it clattered away. Now he would go the way of the boulder, nothing could prevent it.

Deep inside Wayne's head a ringing noise began that went outward into his ears, swallowing up any sane thought he might have had. He was off balance now, his shoes sliding over the polished rocks like so much ice. He flailed his arms madly, attempting to paddle, to stay upright. The noise in his head got louder and merged with the roar from the drift, engulfing him. A familiar picture passed fleetingly before his eyes: Dad, washing at the pump as he did each evening; Mom, lighting the fire in the kitchen range; Sis, playing in the yard. He belonged in that picture. He didn't want to leave it, ever.

"I've got to make it," he said aloud.

In that instant, he became aware of the voice; "If you ever get in a tight spot while wading, *use your rod* as a staff!" His dad was saying it again as he had long ago- one of the bits and pieces of sage advice that lay there, dormant in Wayne's mind until there came that occasion when he would use it.

Quickly his brain grappled with the words, echoed them, tried to interpret them into action. A tight spot. Use your rod. Your rod. *Yes, his rod*; he still had his rod.

Frantically Wayne drove the rod tip with all his might into the bottom of the river. It slipped between the stones easily and held, and his feet automatically grounded themselves seeking a crevice. They found it. He was stopped. He gripped the rod with both hands, sliding one part way down to help weight it. Would it hold? It had to. It was his only chance for survival.

It helped a great deal to be able to think rationally again. He took stock of his position and saw that he was below the marker he had previously set as his goal. He would have to work his way upstream somehow. He'd gotten into a trough, the scoured-out valley that was sometimes present on the upstream side of a bar. He had to get out of the trough. Impossible though the feat appeared, it was the only safe course, if there was such a thing.

He hated to chance pulling the rod. Maybe he'd be unable to force it into the gravel again, but it had to be done. With great effort Wayne surged into the torrential current, at the same instant withdrawing the rod and slamming it back in a new place, all in one coordinated motion. It held, and he gave a gasp of relief. Now he was gaining a small bit of confidence, though he could hardly see where he'd gained much else. He tried it again. Then he rested. Then again, and again. Lunge, stab, rest; lunge, stab, rest. Finally, as he looked toward shore, he felt that with luck he could come out above the deep run.

Wayne was still shaking but the rod was part of him now. In combination with his own wading skill, it was taking him to shore and safety. Soon it was just a little way to go, not over twelve feet. Then it was ten feet, eight feet, six, and he felt the intensity of the current wane ever so slightly, then diminish rapidly. He was beyond danger now. The ordeal was over.

He splashed in to shore, stumbled, then fell forward onto the clean, hard gravel. He pressed his face into it lovingly. After a long while, his head came up and he gazed all around slowly. For a moment he was unable to recognize his surroundings; then the crashing, booming din from the maelstrom below, that had momentarily lulled and at the same time hypnotized him, became the river again.

The strange, *living, breathing* river—alive as surely as the trees, the soil, and the sky. Today the river's heart had been merciful. But she could kill you- quick. Sometimes you needed to be reminded of that.

Wayne pushed himself to his feet. On his cheek, stuck by his dried tears, was the empty, used skin of a stone fly nymph. It came loose and fluttered away flimsily. He felt for his string of fish. It was gone. He'd forgotten about the fish. But it didn't matter, they weren't important now. He held up his rod, the precious bit of steel that had saved his life. The tip was broken off and the guides were mashed.

It didn't matter about that either. He wouldn't be fishing the next day anyway. Not the next day, nor the day after that. Not for a lot of days. The river needed a rest. Later, perhaps, Dad and he would be getting together for that trip to Black Canyon, the one they'd so often talked about. Yes, Wayne was sure they would.

Wesley's note: This part of the Middle Fork of the Willamette River is now deep under the water of Dexter Lake. Donald **Wayne** Murphey— my dad —was a teenager when he made this trial crossing. The Murpheys and Andersons lived in the bottom land that is now buried under Dexter Lake's water in the large inlet south of Highway 58. Don and all his relatives always referred to that inlet as Murphey's Cove because of his parents' old homestead there.

A year after this trial crossing incident, Don's parents—Fred and Judy Murphey (my grandparents)—bought and took over operation of the Williams General Store in Dexter (later renamed Dexter Market). They owned the store from 1937-1945. Judy was Don's stepmother, his sis was step-sister Eileen Murphey who later married Edward Vohs, one of Don's good friends and previously a student at Lowell High School. Don graduated from Pleasant Hill High School in 1939. Eileen graduated from Pleasant Hill in 1942. Don's brother, Jim Murphey, moved in with the Murpheys in Dexter in the summer of 1938 and was a Pleasant Hill 1940 class member. A few insignificant details were changed for this story.

It's appropriate to mention here that when Dad was about thirty he lost his dog while duck hunting on the Willamette River not far from where he made this trial crossing. The black Labrador retriever named "Boy" was swept under a drift pile like the one in this story, and never came up. Dad searched the river downstream of the drift for Boy for quite a while, hoping somehow he would find a way out. Then finally Dad sat on the bank and cried. He always blamed himself for letting Boy go out into the river above the drift.

Don Murphey's brother, Jim Murphey, a Pearl Harbor Survivor, with Don's dog "Boy". *(1947)*

Traffic Line Fur

Wesley Murphey

Driving over 30th Avenue in south Eugene after dark one mid-November evening on my way to a dress rehearsal for the college singing group I belonged to, I spotted a big bushy raccoon lying belly down on the white line at the right edge of my lane. I had a few minutes to spare—not that it would have made any difference—so I pulled onto the shoulder just past the 'coon and turned my car off. This one-hundred-yard stretch of 4-lane highway near Spring Boulevard had been good to me this fall. Assuming it was salvageable, this 'coon would make the third one I'd picked up here in three weeks. In an average week, I drove over 30th Avenue about seven in the morning and again in the early afternoon, Monday through Friday going to or coming from my classes at Eugene Bible College.

The evening traffic rush was over, but there was still a steady flow of cars going past. When I got out of my car, dressed in a three-piece suit and tie, the last thing anyone would have taken me for was a fur trapper. If my car wasn't parked in front of the 'coon, I doubt many people going past would have given the 'coon a second thought either. A passing driver or passenger that saw me walking

142

the short distance back to the 'coon, pointing a flashlight at the pavement, might assume that I was the driver that ran over it. Perhaps they'd even think I just wanted to get it completely out of the roadway, or make sure it was dead.

Unfortunately, when I got to the raccoon it was obvious that, in fact, it wasn't quite dead. Gurgling came from its mouth as it struggled to breath. Its back rose and fell erratically and with great effort. Probably the reason it was straddling the white line was that it had somehow managed to crawl a foot or two after being hit. I waved the light of my flashlight around the grassy edge of the road hoping to find a club-sized stick to finish off the 'coon. There was nothing. I did the only thing I felt I could do— I kicked the 'coon on the top of its head a couple of times with my hard-soled shiny, black dress shoes. It quit gurgling, its back quit rising and falling.

An animal rightist might have considered me a heartless and brutal barbarian. Of course it might have been an animal rightist's car that hit the 'coon and left it in that condition in the first place. I'm sure they, like everybody else who drives a motor vehicle, occasionally run over a wild animal or domestic pet, killing it or— like this 'coon—maiming it. There was little doubt in my mind that the 'coon would have died within the hour, but I had the means to hasten the inevitable and end the animal's misery, so I did.

I looked its bushy body over where it lay, then used a hand on one of its legs to turn it over to see if there was visible damage on the underside. There were no obvious injuries to the 'coon's body or head; however, there was some blood around its mouth. I deduced that its lungs had been damaged. I knew from past experience with road-killed furbearers, that the injuries hidden underneath the skin and internally could be extensive.

There was a short break in traffic, so I quickly picked up the 'coon by a back leg and carried it the thirty feet to my car. I opened my trunk lid, then set the 'coon on some newspaper that I always kept in the back, just in case. I walked over to the grass at the edge of the road and ripped off a handful to wipe my hands.

When I got to the college, I immediately washed my hands in the restroom before proceeding to the stage to warm up my voice with the other nine singers and the director. I told a couple of the guys about the 'coon. They laughed, but they already knew I was a trapper and avid hunter, so my picking up the 'coon was no surprise to them. I had already earned the nickname, "Beaver Breath." Several of my buddies liked to tease me about the beaver spaghetti or tacos I made with ground beaver meat. But they were also quick to try a piece of raccoon or beaver jerky whenever I had some with me.

Back then, prices were good for practically all furbearer pelts. The raccoon I picked up that day was fully prime, but the earlier ones were unprime—so-called "blue 'coons." At the fur sale, I sold the first two 'coons from 30th Avenue for $15 each; the big prime one brought $30.

A gallon of gasoline was only going for about $1 in my area then. A guy could have run a pretty lucrative fur line on certain highways without ever setting a trap—especially at first light after a warm rainy night.

When prices were good, back in the 1980s, I'd pick up any dead raccoon I saw on the road from mid-October through early March, as long as it wasn't too badly mangled. I'd even pick up nutrias sometimes. Like many trappers, I was always on the lookout for some "highway trapped fur," though I didn't bother with skunks or opossums. In the heyday of fur prices, the first trapper over a given stretch of road on a winter morning had the best chance of "catching" fur from the night's traffic line. You'd rarely see a dead 'coon after 8 a.m. unless you happened to be that first trapper. Fur prices for species like raccoon and nutria have been poor for so long now that I can't remember the last time I picked up a dead animal off the highway.

Just like that short span of highway that claims multiple deer over a given period of time, a trapper knows that seeing more than one furbearer in a certain stretch of road can indicate an animal expressway. The 30th Avenue section near Spring Boulevard was just such a crossing for raccoons. Although I never saw two dead 'coons *there* in one day, more than once, *on some other highway*, I've seen what I called a massacre when a momma 'coon and two or three young 'coons were laying dead within twenty-five feet of each other. I don't know whether they were all hit at the same time, by the same vehicle, or perhaps when investigating the death of one of their family members shortly before. It always saddens me to see that situation.

Crossin' the highway late last night, he should a....

Lest anyone think the animals that I—or other trappers—picked up off the road were easy money, I can assure you that it was rarely any fun to skin them out. If I was lucky, the animal was only hit in the head. In that case I would only have to deal with a crushed skull with brains falling out when I skinned out the head. Often, the animal's body was crushed, and the guts and blood would come pouring out as soon as I peeled the skin down a ways. I wrapped a lot of toilet paper around damaged carcasses of road-killed animals to contain the mess as I worked to free the pelt. Then I had to work extra hard when I fleshed the pelt's leather to scrape the excessive blood out of it.

A few days after picking up the first road-killed raccoon off of 30th Avenue in 1980, I happened to be standing behind my vehicle alongside a gravel road in the hills near Marcola, north of Springfield, in-between deer hunts, when a game warden came along in his white Dodge Ram pickup. For whatever reason, I had the trunk open on my 1971 Dodge Polara. The warden stopped in the middle of the road just behind my car and asked what I was doing. When I said deer hunting, he got out of his truck and asked to see my hunting license and blacktail deer tag. While I was digging out my wallet to get the requested items, he leaned over my bumper and looked into the trunk.

"What's this blood from?" he asked, immediately suspicious.

"It's from a road-killed raccoon I picked up a few days ago on 30th Avenue," I answered, while handing him my license and tag. "I'm a fur trapper."

"Do you have your trapping license on you?"

"Yes, I do. But I'm not doing any trapping yet."

The only seasons opened yet, were red fox and coyote. I was pretty sure he wouldn't give me any problem over picking up a road-killed 'coon.

He looked at my hunting license and deer tag, but didn't ask to see my trapping license. Satisfied, he handed the items back to me.

"I don't think you're going to be doing much trapping," he said. "From all the feedback I'm getting around the office and from what other troopers are hearing, the consensus is that Measure 5 will easily pass this week."

"I hope you're wrong. If it does pass I guess you guys will have one less thing to keep up on, won't you?" I said rhetorically. "From all I'm hearing, I think the measure's going down. I want to believe that Oregonians are too smart to buy the animal rights' propaganda."

"I hope you're right," he said. "What animals do you trap?"

"Water animals. I haven't done anything with cats or coyotes yet."

"Well, I hope you get to keep trapping," he said, as he got back in the Ram. "Are you seeing any deer up here?"

"Haven't seen any today. This is the first time I've hunted up here. I usually hunt up around Lookout Point Reservoir."

"Well good luck," he said, starting his truck.

"Thanks."

Fortunately the game warden was wrong and I was right. Oregon's *Ballot Measure 5* was defeated 63% to 37% a few days later. Then in 2000, another anti-trapping measure, *#97*, was defeated by Oregon voters 59% to 41%.

Now the animal rights groups are at it again, trying to get a measure on the 2014 general election ballot that would ban all fur trapping, and almost all damage-control trapping in Oregon. The animal rights wackos are going after trappers because they are the smallest animal-user group and the animal rightists were successful in getting trapping banned or severely restricted in a couple of Oregon's neighboring states—Washington and California.

But **BEWARE**— the ultimate goal of most of these animal rights groups is to put animals on an equal level with humans and to shut down **all** consumptive uses of **all** animals. This includes banning all trapping, hunting and fishing, and all animal farming including raising animals for any consumptive purpose, especially for eating.

If you've noticed more raccoons and other fur-bearing animals lying along the road in your area in recent years, you can be sure that poor fur prices are a contributing factor. Not only are there fewer trappers setting traps for critters, but there are also very few that pick them up off the road anymore. If trapping is banned entirely, the number of animals killed on roadways will increase even further. Of course the dead carcasses will be picked over by crows, ravens, buzzards and other birds, animals and insects. Very little goes to waste in nature's circle of life.

It's a shame when man isn't allowed to perform his proper role at the top of nature's food chain. Enjoy your steak in your favorite restaurant. Someone had to kill that animal so you could. And a rancher had to raise it first. Anyone who eats meat is actually not so different from a farmer or trapper, just farther removed from nature's circle of life.

Murphey boys and friend with Fern Ridge crappies 1962.

Crappies
The Black and White of It

Don Murphey

Crappies in the Far West, like those anywhere,
need a full bag of tricks.

It was early March, and I was fishing through a blustering wind-storm that every half an hour or so drove a cutting drizzle into my face. Between showers the wind was drying my clothes, which kept me feeling somewhat like a refrigerator. But I could take it. A walloping big crappie was socking my bucktail every few casts, and each time I felt that familiar tug on the leader I laughed. I laughed at weather reports, fishing predictions, and water that was too muddy, too cold, and entirely too rough to fish.

It was impossible to lay out a straight fly line in that wind, but by quartering my casts I managed to get my bucktail blown against the steep, rocky shoreline down the lake a little way. This handicap is what led me to the big crappies. Strikes came when I retrieved the fly in short jerks parallel to the rocks.

The water had been stirred up so much by the wind that its color was an opaque brown; in fact one fisherman had told me it was too muddy to fish. But right along shore and extending a few inches out, the water was fairly clear—something I'd never noticed before— and the crappies were lying on the edge of this clearer margin ready to nab anything the wind or waves swept against the shore. It was just one of many little discoveries that have helped put crappies in my creel.

Crappies are notably vulnerable in spring, but it should never be said they are easy to catch. True, there are days when crappies go wild and seem to strike any and everything you cast, but there are many more days when most fishermen give up and go fishless on the basis of any number of tried-and-true excuse theories.

It took me years to learn that in the spring crappies seldom act exactly the same two days in a row. If you were catching them yesterday with a slow, steady retrieve at a distance from shore, today you'd better try them with a close-in, short-jerk retrieve. Occasionally I'll even hit my favorite spot on that rare spring even- ing when crappies are slam-banging a fast-skimming surface fly. It doesn't happen nearly often enough, but when it does it's something to remember—especially if the fish are large.

They were running large one evening a few years ago when my brother Jim and I were fishing Fern Ridge Reservoir, 10 miles west of Eugene, Oregon. That's not far from the country community of Pleasant Hill, where I live and work as a bus driver for the local schools and also travel a 70-mile mail route. My brother is an auto- motive electrician and lives in Springfield, which is also nearby. We'd fished several hours along a railroad fill where rising dam waters lapped a rocky shore, and we hadn't had much luck. The crappies were there, we knew, for we'd taken them regularly in previous weeks. It was getting dark and we were ready to quit unless things began to change fast. Then, suddenly, they did.

The water began to boil all along the rocks, right in close, and a gentle breeze stirred where all had been quiet. Then fish began to break as far down the lake as we could see, and the plop, plop sound of it was wonderful to hear.

"Are they crappies?" Jim called from a distance.

"They don't act like it," I answered. After about 20 minutes of frustrating casting I began to wonder if the fish weren't carp.

Finally Jim turned the trick. "Hey, there's one of 'em," he shouted as his spinning rod developed a bend. "It's a good fish, whatever it is."

I stopped fishing and walked toward him.

"It's a crappie all right," Jim said. "Man, look at the size." He was lifting the fish out. "Got him on a fast retrieve."

I cast, doubled the speed of my retrieve, and drew a big splash with a crappie inside. The fish zipped out from shore, boiled the surface a few times, then went deep and pulled my fly rod down hard. In a minute or two it was circling close, and finally I got my thumb in its mouth. After that, the strikes came every couple of casts. The crappies wanted the fly on top and they wanted it to move in long sweeping pulls. Those silvery slabs almost came right out on the bank after our bucktails and not one was under a pound.

Crappies don't often strike a fast retrieve. Usually it's the ultra-slow retrieve that kills, and about 90 percent of the time that you're not catching fish while someone next to you is, you'll find you're going too fast. Again, crappies don't often strike at the surface. Mostly you fish your lure near bottom, though in the spring this sometimes means water only a couple of feet deep. But when the usual method fails, try it shallow and fast.

If you're new at the crappie game, then you need to know that in the spring crappies gather in shallow water to spawn. However, they start migrating toward the shallows long before they actually spawn. In western Oregon, we start catching hungry, migrating crappies in February, and we have them in the shallow at least through May, the spawning month.

White crappies from Fern Ridge Reservoir, Oregon.

Finding these spring crappies is no problem at the most popular spots, for almost always there are crowds of fishermen to follow. Though crappie fishermen generally are secretive, they can hardly escape you in the spring. There are too many of them. But if you must search the fish out for yourself, look to the inlets of the river or lake. Crappies love flooded, fertile pasture land. If you find a cove where water has flooded back into the willows, look no further; if it's shallow—not over four or five feet—you've likely found the ideal spawning ground.

Now for baits. When you think of crappies you should think of minnows. Minnows are the best live bait, worms the worst. The types of artificial baits that catch crappies are legion, and what works in one area will surely work in another— depending on how

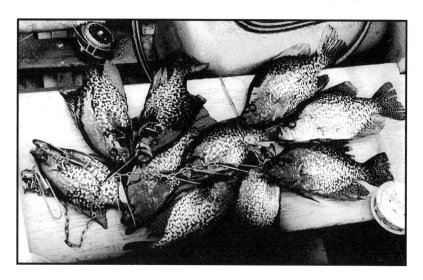

Black Crappies from Siltcoos Lake, Oregon

the angler uses it. All good crappie lures have one thing in common, though; they're small, not over two inches long. To get on the right wave length for crappies you must tune in with the right size lure.

In the spring you never need to use live bait unless you prefer to. I have plenty of fun and success using a fly rod and bucktails. The pattern isn't important; have some light flies and some dark. Though most fishermen favor a white or yellow pattern, I've had the best luck on dark colors, especially during overcast, showery, spring days. I don't like to use any weight, but a sinking line helps.

Spinning rigs almost invariably feature the lure hanging two or three feet under a bobber. When plain bucktails are used, a split shot helps casting. The bubble often attracts crappies, and at times this is a distinct advantage. Where most spin fisherman fall, however, is in not varying the rate or style of retrieve. Often the novice, who enjoys the long casts that are possible, overshoots the crappie area that's in close to shore, and hits only the barren spots. On the other hand, he can reach distant hotspots not accessible with a fly rod.

Whether fishing from boat or shore, you'll usually find that most spring crappies hug the banks. Casting and retrieving parallel to shore is often the only way you can get strikes. Sometimes you need to bounce the lure off bottom; crappies take right after the bounce. But if you're not willing to deviate from some certain twist that paid off for you once or twice before, don't expect to catch crappies consistently.

Here are two good retrieves: 1. Make a fairly long cast, let the fly or lure sink, then start it coming toward you in long sweeps and slight pauses. Make the pauses just long enough to keep the lure down, the sweeps to cover three or four feet at a time. When the lure is just a few feet from shore or boat, stop it, let stay where it is, and pretend it is a little bell. Start tinkling that bell by twitching your rod tip in about the same cadence as that made by the second hand on a clock. Then's when the crappie hits.   2. This retrieve—which often will induce crappies to strike when persons tell you they aren't hitting—can be used in combination with No. 1. But instead of tinkling the bell, or just after tinkling it, swim the lure off at right angles for a few feet. Then suddenly turn it about and swim it back. Crappies strike just after the turn.

Crappies are most difficult to catch in summer. Locating them seems to be the big problem. Drawing on memory, I recall that when I was a boy I caught crappies throughout the hot summers after I discovered that crappies and shade go together like ham and eggs. I lived in Portland then, that Oregon city on the lower Willamette River. The area wasn't exactly a fishing paradise in those early 30s, for pollution was fast wrecking the salmon fishery. Yet there was some great crappie fishing.

In my neighborhood there was another kid who loved crappie fishing as much as I did, and it would be hard to calculate the hours and days we spent scouting the outskirts of the city for good spots. During those few years we stored a wealth of fishing lore that I tap to good advantage today. Clarence and I would board an early morning streetcar with our rods and lunches. We'd always have to transfer once or twice to another line before reaching our destination, some little-known spot along the Columbia or Willamette rivers. Fishing-wise we knew those trolley lines like the backs of our hands, and something I'll always remember as wonderful went out of Portland when the streetcars died a few years later.

White and black crappies had been firmly established in our area since the early 1900s, and Clarence and I had somehow made the amazing deduction that the whites liked to hang around large rocks while the blacks had an affinity for floating logs.

I can't remember if we ever proved that theory, but I recall one of our outstanding crappie holes. It was at a slow, deep place on the Willamette where a railroad spur ran on pilings out into the river for a way. At the end of the spur was an ancient structure with red sidings, and it was under this that we caught our crappies. We called it "the redhouse."

A bracework of planks had been spiked to the forest of pilings beneath the redhouse, and it was dark under there. Working your way around was no small feat, but it was well worth the trouble. Crappies were always there—probably by the thousands. They liked the shade; and they liked those pilings, which of course meant food. Plankton around water-soaked pilings always attracts minnows.

Minnows then, as now, were standard crappie bait, but we never used them. We weren't equipped to gather minnows even if they'd been easy to get. Furthermore, we never needed them. The first crappie that was caught was sacrificed for bait. Catching the first one was the hardest part, but we found it could be done with a worm and lots of patience.

This cut bait was popularly called white-meat. It wasn't much good when used in a chunk, but sliced into thin, tapered ribbons it was deadly. The crappie itself makes the best bait, especially the silvery sides and belly. The strip is hooked through the widest end—push the hook's point through the meat, then the skin—and hangs loosely on the bend of the hook. You fished it until it began to get ragged, then replaced it with a fresh strip. We eliminated weights and bobbers so the slightest movement of our rod tips would make the strip seem alive. Needless to say, it resembled a live minnow.

Probably every crappie water of consequence in the country has a "redhouse." Of course, it may not look exactly like ours. It may take the shape of a bridge, or a dock, but the essentials are there: shade and pilings.

Ever notice how crappies like to school up under an anchored boat? Imagine, then, a blanket of shade covering perhaps an acre or more of water. That's what you have when you come by a moored raft of logs. The bottom side of that raft is Grand Central Station in crappieland. You catch them on the hottest days from the log rafts.

Clarence and I used the same procedure fishing from rafts as we did under the redhouse. Strip bait was our meat, and it always worked. We'd look for an extra big log, preferably one with a deformed butt, one with maybe a long rot seam that was slightly hollowed out—a place to hold our lunches so we wouldn't lose them. We'd sink our little strips through a crack between the logs, and as soon as it reached the underside we'd swim it along minnow-like. We'd feel a light tap, then there'd be that characteristic run, and up would come a crappie.

Getting out on these rafts was sometimes a ticklish business, for often we had to walk a slender, water-filled boom log. More than once the cost of getting out there amounted to water-soaked clothes, but who cared about such trivia at 13 years old in the summertime, with crappies in the offing?

Oddly enough, hopping about on or even rolling the logs never bothers these schools of crappies. They may briefly sink down a few feet but they come right back. The narrowest cracks make for the best fishing because less light penetrates. Another tip: hang a stringer of crappies in one of these openings and fish near these live decoys.

"ONE MORE FOR THE STRINGER"

There is a fall crappie run. Actually it's a feeding binge rather than a run. The fish are found in shallows again, as in the spring, after the days get cooler and shorter. They gorge on minnows and little else, often driving the little baitfish to the surface much like ocean game fish. At this time of year in this state—where minnows are illegal— I forget about artificial and use only the white-meat strip. Pork rind isn't a tenth as good. The deadliness of the strip cannot be over-stressed. I've seen it score too many times to believe otherwise, yet few fishermen use or know about it.

Last winter I took my kids fishing at the tail-waters of a crappie reservoir. It was one of those not uncommon balmy days between Pacific storms, and my mouth watered for fresh crappie fillets. Apparently a lot of others had the same craving, for fishermen's cars were parked all over.

The kids and I took up a position alongside two older gentlemen who had been fishing all day with worms. They had three crappies in a bucket. While I always consider it a challenge to catch that first crappie I intend to sacrifice for bait, this day I'd cheated and brought a small one from the freezer where I'd kept it for such a purpose. I provided my own two older children and a neighbor boy with strips and set about rigging my own tackle. Before I finished the kids were hauling in crappies. I joined them, and we never stopped until one creel and one stringer were filled. It took two hours.

The two old gentlemen suffered through the whole thing with good-natured encouragement for the kids, without themselves having a bite. They were too proud, I suppose, to ask how it was done. From where I stood I could see at least 25 persons, and most of them were using jigs or worms. As near as I could tell, only one other person caught anything while we were there, and that was a single small crappie. It was one more case out of dozens when the white-meat strip won out.

While most outdoor writers are hip to the fine crappie fishing available in the Far West, you still see it implied in print occasionally that good crappie fishing ends somewhere east of the Rockies. But it seems to me that no matter where in the U.S. you happen to be, there is bound to be some mighty handy crappie water. Just remember, when you fish it, that one bucket of minnows doesn't necessarily equal one bucket of crappies. Through all seasons it takes a full bag of tricks. Never, never say crappies are easy to catch.

Wesley's note- This article was published in Outdoor Life in 1962 under the title "Black and White of It." Fishing laws have changed a lot since then, though using live minnows in inland waters was illegal in Oregon and many states even then. Some undesirable minnow and trash fish populations in many bodies were caused by live "minnows" escaping fishermen's hooks and reproducing in waters not native to them.

In this crappie article, my dad (Don Murphey) spoke of fishing in Portland during the summer when he was a young teenager. Each year from 1933 through 1936, Dad and his brother Jim spent part of each summer with their father, step-mother and two younger siblings at their homestead located between Dexter and Lowell, and part of the summer in Portland, where they lived permanently with their mom and little sister. Of course, being the fishing fanatic that he was, Dad fished every possible chance he got wherever he was, whether in Portland or Dexter-Lowell. In the summer of 1937, Dad moved down to his father's place in Dexter for good. Brother Jim did so in 1938. The Murpheys' old homestead was buried under the water of Dexter Lake when Dexter Reservoir was filled in 1954.

Murphey gang camped at Salmon Creek, Oregon. (1975)
Left to Right: Eileen (Murphey) Vohs, Ed Vohs, Jim, Becky, Rosella
and Gerry Murphey. (Don Murphey is taking photo.)

Trapping Season 1998-99

Wesley Murphey

In late November, before beginning my own line, I set three otter traps on a tributary to Letz Creek, tributary of the Siuslaw River, west of Lorane, Oregon for the Northwest Steelheaders, who had contacted the ODFW. Turned out the guy I dealt with who was in charge of the Steelheader's operation on Letz Creek was Daryl Hober, one of my dad's old mail patrons up Lost Creek. Two of his daughters and his son were in successive classes right behind me at Pleasant Hill. Sadly, during the winter, Daryl died of a massive heart attack. Because of that I was never able to recover the three #600 Montgomery traps I had given him to use after I pulled out. No one had any idea where they were.

After I set the otter traps, I showed Daryl where they were so he could check them, saving me time and mileage; I caught one big otter in about 14 days. Because otters are nomadic and may not return to the same small creek for a couple weeks or more, I could only do so much in the time I had. In retrospect, I probably should have set several traps in Letz Creek itself, in addition to the three traps I set in the inlet and outlet to their little pond.

I'll get started on foot, before picking up the drift boat I've lined up. I should add that I've been taking 8 credit hours of classes at Lane Community College this fall (Nutrition, 4 hrs, Human Anatomy and Physiology I, 4 hrs). I will only be taking 4 credit hours after winter break. The anatomy class requires a huge amount of memorization and has several mid-term exams plus the final. These classes will count toward the Dental Hygiene Program that I will apply to get into down the road.

Dec 16, Wed- I set 15 traps at Larry Shrenk's (Lane County Sheriff's deputy) off of Cloverdale Road. Weather is turning cold. Finished my finals at LCC yesterday.

Dec 18, Fri- Got 6 nutrias and 1 medium beaver. Pulled 10 sets from Shrenks, put in 39 sets at Harrolds' Dairy Farm northeast of Creswell.

Dec 19, Sat- Frigid weather, low teens at night, day-time highs in mid-20s. I only checked Harrolds, had 18 nutria and a large medium beaver. Had a #330 stolen from slough adjoining Coast Fork River at back of Harrolds. Probably a duck hunter. Added 3 sets.

Dec 21, Mon- Pulled 5 remaining traps at Shrenks, all full: an otter and 4 nutrias. At Harrolds, I caught 11 nutrias, 1 raccoon and 1 skunk. I pulled a lot of the traps at Harrolds to be used on McKenzie River tomorrow.

Dec 22, Tue- Frigid weather continues. Put in 40 sets on Bellinger to Hayden Bridge run. Hayden Rapids were a piece of cake.

Dec 23, Wed- Pulled remaining traps at Harrolds, caught 6 nutrias.

Dec 24, Thur- Finally warmed to above freezing during day. Caught 8 beavers and 3 nutes on Mac., added about 10 sets.

Dec 25, Merry Christmas. Happy Birthday, Jesus.

Dec 26, Sat- A very good day: 9 beavers (including a 66 pounder), 5 otters, 7 nutrias and a grey fox. Rain.

Wes on his trapline with the kids, Cody and Tasha.
Middle Fork of the Willamette River. (February 15, 1999)

Dec 27-30 Heavy rain, high temps, mountain snow melt, McKenzie at full bank, couldn't get on it. No doubt almost all my traps are way under water.

Dec 31, Thurs- Water still way up, though not bank full now. Took a chance, was able to recover all but 9 traps. Had 4 beavers, 3 nutrias and a muskrat. Catch to date: 23 beavers, 59 nutes, 7 otters, and 1 each: coon, skunk, grey fox, muskrat.

Jan 1-3 Waiting out high water. Back to college this week on Tuesdays and Thursdays, taking Human Anatomy & Phys. II. (Only 4 credit hours this term.) Will run line M,W,Fri and Sat or Sunday.

Jan 4, Mon- Ran Mac, water still high. I set some traps, but still couldn't get some from earlier. No animals in those I could recover—mostly sprung and fouled with debris.

Jan 6, Wed- River still high. Catch: 1 blanket beaver, 1 otter and 5 nutes. The beaver was caught in trap I couldn't reach before. Fur not slipping yet; I skinned and boarded hide this evening, pointed a fan directly at it. I'm very discouraged.

Jan 8, Fri- 4 beavers, 3 nutes.

Jan 10, Sun- Pulled McKenzie line; caught 6 beavers, 2 otters, 3 nutes and 1 coon.

Jan 11, Mon- Got 38 sets on Willamette River, Beltline to Hileman Park. Water is a bit high (good level for trapping). Good beaver and otter sign.

Jan 13, Wed- Great day, the kind you dream of with most traps full! Caught 12 beavers, 15 nutrias and 1 otter. All but one of the beavers were big, mostly superblankets (XXXL).

Jan 15, Fri- Lots of rain. River way up, pulled line. Picked up 5 beavers, 16 nutes, and 2 otters. Season totals to date: 51 beavers, 101 nutrias, 13 otters, 2 coons, and 1 each of those mentioned earlier.

Jan 16-19 Heavy rain.

Jan 20, Wed- Put in 18 sets on foot at Harrolds, lots of rain, water way up.

Jan 22, Fri- 2 beavers, 1 otter, 7 nutes and a 'possum. Weather turning dry and warm, but will take some time to get rivers down to trappable level as the Army Corps will be bringing reservoir levels down.

Jan 24, Sun- Caught 1 beaver, 1 otter, 8 nutes and 1 grey fox.

A good day on the trapline.

Jan 27, Wed- 2 beavers, 15 nutes, 1 coon. Put in 15 sets behind Bring's Recycling. Someone already trapped here earlier, judging by some conibear support sticks left in place.

Jan 29, Fri- 1 beaver, 11 nutes (only 2 from Brings, obviously thinned out earlier by other trapper). Pulled Harrolds lower, will pull Bring traps Sunday and get started back on Willamette River Monday.

Jan 31, Sun- 1 beaver, 5 nutes and 1 skunk. Pulled traps.

Feb 3, Wed- Other commitments kept me off river until today. Set 42 traps back on Beltline-Hileman Run on Willamette River. Water is low, but was able to get down left channel just above Hileman.

Feb 5, Fri- Today's catch was 5 beavers, 14 nutrias, an otter, coon, and a muskrat. Was sprinkling part of the day.

Eugene contractor friend Mark Adkins along with me on river today with his camcorder. Before trapping season started, I was selected by John Kulish, owner/ designer of Species Specific Traps, to be included in a national trapping video with 7 other trappers. The video was to be a how-to, but also as a tool to promote his species specific separator series of killer traps. He sent me 4 dozen free (24 each of 10" by 10"s and 10 by 12s) before the season. I already have some video footage from the past, but the footage we got today included some sets and results with the Specie Specific traps as well as other Victor, Montgomery and BMI models I use. I will have the footage professionally edited before sending it to John Kulish sometime after the season. I know I was selected because of the articles I've had published in The Trapper and Predator Caller magazine; John wants my endorsement.

(Note added in 2013- I ended up donating all but a few of the dislocator traps over the years to the Oregon Trappers auction at the annual Waldo Lake Trappers Rendezvous. Personally, I didn't favor them. They take up more room, they are less handy to carry by hand because of the gap between jaws and I can't see that they kill the animal any faster. I do like their trigger system though, and have adopted it on traps when their existing triggers wore out. As of this date, I've never seen the trapping video I was featured in. But Carl Berg, the most prolific beaver and otter trapper in Oregon, and my good friend, told me that John Kulish told him that the video footage John received from me was the best he received for actually showing and explaining how-to put in certain sets. I still have the unedited footage that Mark took that day.)

Feb 7 Heavy rain last two nights, waiting until tomorrow to try to retrieve my traps.

Feb 8, Mon- Water way high. Retrieved all but 2 traps, which are just above Hileman Landing. Caught 4 beavers, 2 otters and 8 nutes. **Totals to date**: 67 beavers, 169 nutes, 18 otters, 4 coons, 3 muskrats, 2 grey fox, 2 skunks and 1 opossum.

Feb 10, Wed- Got in 36 sets in Pengra to Jasper run on Willamette Middle Fork. Water is high, but not as bad as Beltline to Hileman run (which also includes water from reservoirs on the Coast Fork of the Willamette and the McKenzie River.)

The fill cycle on the Middle Fork reservoirs (Fall Creek, Hills Creek and Lookout Point) began Feb 1st, so now they don't have to dump out all the water that comes into those reservoirs. They have specific water levels that they want to achieve by certain dates with the goal of having the reservoirs full for the start of summer. Several factors come into play in the Army Corps determination of what the water level needs to be at a given date in order to get the reservoirs full, yet still provide the flood control capabilities throughout the late winter and spring rainy season and snow melt season. One of the key factors is the amount and makeup (water content) of the mountain snowpack in the upper end of these watersheds.

Feb 12, Fri- Took an older teenage boy, Tom, on line with me today. He really enjoyed the experience and my good catch impressed him: 11 beavers, 3 otters, 4 nutrias and 1 raccoon. Between the weight of the catch, combined with Tom's and my weight, maneuvering the boat on lower end of run was somewhat difficult. The water level being a little high made this easier, and of course the lower end, below Fall Creek's confluence, is easier boating anyway than some other places. I drove over to Hileman after I dropped the boat off at home, and was able to hike in and retrieve the traps that I couldn't get to the other day. Had a nutria there as well.

Feb 13, Sat- Set Clearwater to Island Park run, 22 sets.

Feb 14, Sunday- Ran Pengra-Jasper run after church and pulled all traps. Caught 4 beavers, 4 nutes and 2 otters.

Feb 15, Mon- Took my kids, Cody (10) and Tasha (almost 8) on Clearwater-Island Park river line today. Had 6 beavers and 3 nutes.

Feb 17, Wed- Picked 7 beavers, 1 otter, 2 nutrias, 1 mink and 1 muskrat

Feb 19, Fri- Pulled line, am done for year. Caught 9 beavers, and 1 otter.

After we got home and unloaded the boat, I took Cody over to a slough near our house and helped him put in 2 nutria traps. During the season when I'm trying to make a living, I can't take the time to do this very much. With him being mostly blind, he can't just take off on his bike with some traps and go set some place on his own like a sighted person could.

Feb 20 to 22, checked both traps daily, Tasha went along a couple times- Cody caught 4 nutrias. Like every other trapper I know, Cody loves the anticipation of checking, and the reward of having animals in, his traps.

Feb 22- I took all my otters to Springfield ODFW and got them tagged.

My final season totals: 104 beavers, 25 otters, 183 nutrias, 5 raccoons, 4 muskrats, 2 grey fox, 2 skunks, 1 mink, and 1 opossum.

The constant high water conditions made this my hardest winter yet for trapping the rivers. I could have caught a lot more critters if I had been more inclined to go trap some back up areas— like Ellisons (which I didn't trap at all this year)— away from the river when the rivers were too high to trap. Obviously going to school really put a dent in my flexibility and took a lot of time too.

*Cody and Tasha Murphey with a couple of nutrias
on Cody's trapline. (February 1999)*

*Marshall Lee Murphey with a nutria and a raccoon caught
on his Uncle Wes Murphey's trapline January 1981.*

Making Friends
with the Shaggy Mane

Don Murphey

The field had once been the receptacle for ash, charcoal and odd splinters of partly burned raw fir planks that spilled from the waste conveyor of a saw mill of the early 1930s. Even now, after years of regeneration, it still had a ways to go to reach minimum cow pasture. Yet it was beautiful in autumn, for it had shaggy manes by the thousands.

Driving by the field one day in 1960, I spied patches of white on a dark background and did a double-take. In minutes, I was at the door of the owner.

"Buddy," I said to Bill Johnson, the owner of the field, "you've got a gold mine out there! And if you don't mind, ah—"

"Go ahead and pick 'em," Bill replied, "and I'll tell you what; if you're still alive tomorrow, I'll know they're safe and will gather a batch of mushrooms myself."

He needn't have worried, for identifying the shaggy mane is foolproof. The white closed umbrella, the dark brown spot on top, the multiple fringes or shags from whence it gets its name all are unmistakable. Do, however, avoid the buttons—the beginning stages— to prevent a stray poisonous variety of a different species from getting mixed in with the shaggy manes.

It's not often you find the finest member of the coprinus species of edible mushroom in such numbers. Usually this seemingly shy fungus will send up only a tantalizing sample for you, perhaps a couple dozen stalks at the most in its rather limited habitat.

Our family drives a lot of country roads, and we've found the hard-packed borders, right on the gravel shoulders, to be a place to watch for shaggy manes. Another good bet is any spot that has been filled in with river loam. Mixed in with this loam, and of course not discernible to the eye, are a lot of rotting remnants of cottonwood limbs either from trimming or from windfall. When the right stage of decomposition sets in there will be shaggy manes in the vicinity, their mycelium (roots) feeding on the decaying wood.

Lawns produce some Coprinus, but more often than not they are one of the three other kinds, the eating qualities of which are either in question or inferior. We've seen a few good clumps of Coprinus comatus, the shaggy mane, on lawns.

Shaggy Manes

Finally, we prefer a place—not generally listed in the mushroom book— where, if you hit it during the right stage in its old age, a veritable treasure can be collected: an old fir sawmill site. The bonanza in Bill Johnson's field has now passed its zenith. Three years ago, in early November before the main frosts, there was still a bushel to be had. Last year there were just a few scattered stalks. But surely there are other old sawmill sites still to be found.

When you find shaggy manes it's best to cut them off at ground level with a knife and avoid the earth and debris they grow in. Stay away from those turning black, but a touch of pinkish on the lower edge of the gills doesn't hurt provided you eat them soon after.

Never store them in your refrigerator overnight; the process of turning to ink will already have begun. The popular name, inky caps, has good reasoning behind it. Shaggy manes turn to blackish ink soon after they mature or are picked. Twenty-four hours is about the maximum for storing, and this in a dry place with the mushrooms separated.

Scrape the caps off with fingernail or knife blade during washing or before. Giant specimens up to eight inches are every bit as good as the small ones. Their stems may be split lengthwise and used, but the big ones require longer cooking.

Fry the shaggy manes in butter and expect a lot of their bulk to turn into juice. They will need a sprinkling of salt but no pepper; they're peppery by nature. And get ready for a little bit of heaven on a plate!

Wesley's note- I've eaten a couple dozen varieties of mushrooms. Shaggy Manes are without a doubt my favorite. As Dad said, you can't keep them overnight uncooked in your refrigerator. However, if you cook them, they will keep in your fridge for at least a couple of days. I don't know beyond that, they've always been eaten by then.

Warning: As related in this story, land owner Bill Johnson made the comment, "If you're still alive in the morning …"

This is a misconception about mushroom poisoning. The symptoms of poisoning from some of the deadliest mushrooms may not even show up in the first 24 hours. But then over the next several days the victim begins experiencing a series of symptoms that gradually escalate. Without immediate and ongoing medical intervention, and possibly a kidney or liver transplant, the person will likely die.

Although only a few mushroom species are deadly—most toxic varieties cause temporary mild-to-severe gastro-intestinal problems, hallucinations, delirium etc.—no person should eat a mushroom without being certain it is edible. Fortunately, many varieties, like Shaggy Manes, are easy to identify. The Murphey family has enjoyed eating a variety of wild mushrooms as long as I can remember.

If you do hunt wild mushrooms, get a good mushroom field guide and go with an experienced mushroom hunter.

Hunting Buddy "Bear"

Wesley Murphey

As I finish stuffing my daypack with a change of clean clothes, my nose picks up an all-too-familiar odor. Bear has arrived.

Bear and I have been best friends since we met years ago. When I nicknamed him *Bear* a few years later, he thought it was because I admired his hunting ability. Truth is it was because he smells like an old boar. I doubt he's spent thirty dollars on soap in all the years I've known him.

I enjoy Bear's company when we're out in wide open spaces and I can stay upwind of him. The tough part for me is getting there. Whether we ride in his truck or mine, I hold my breath for as long as I can and then inhale through my mouth in order to bypass my olfactory senses as much as possible. This strategy works all right on the short rides—under ten minutes—because I can get by on about one breath per minute. It's the long rides that get to me.

On a few occasions I've awakened to find myself lying on gravel or dirt beside the truck with him bent down over me blowing his bear-meat breath into my face. He tells me I passed out and he's worried about me. I tell him, "I don't have any health problems; I just need some fresh air."

Bear's latest hunting fad is to carry a five pound bottle of cow elk urine with him and spray himself down every fifteen minutes or so. On a recent bow hunting trip—we just took up bow hunting last year—he doused himself to start the day and said,

"Let me spray some on you."

"No thanks," I said, "I won't be more than a mile away from you. You've got enough on to cover my odor at that distance."

"Come on, just a little bit," he insists.

"Look Bear, you smell like a barnyard! Yesterday I ended up with a pounding headache from walking near you and breathing fumes. Then when we stopped to eat, I couldn't taste the ham and cheese in my sandwiches or the nuts and caramel in my Pay Day. All's I could smell was that rancid cow elk pee. You thought I walked up that little ridge with my last sandwich to scout for elk sign. In fact, it was to get some fresh air. I don't know how you can stand it!"

"It's not that bad."

"You don't have a clue, do you?" I went on. "Do you want to know the real reason I don't bring my canvas tent when we hunt together? I'm not sure I'd live through the night inhaling all the putrid odors emanating from you and your clothes. You crawl right into your bag without changing or washing off. The one thing that surprises me is that you don't spray yourself down with that elk pee before you go to bed."

"Maybe I should. It's obvious you don't care about my feelings."

"I didn't mean to hurt your feelings. I was just trying to get the point across. Besides, I'm sure that cow-elk urine doesn't increase your chances by more than five percent."

"If it only increases my chances by *one percent*, I'll stand behind a cow elk and let her drench me."

"Well, you go ahead and increase your chances by one percent. I'll rely on my hunting skill to get my elk."

"I'll take any edge I can get," he said, getting the last word in as usual.

There's something about being in the woods that always gets Bear's bowels moving. Like clockwork, half an hour after we leave the pickup, Bear will ask, "Do you have any toilet paper?" By then we're already half a mile from the truck and he's reached the point where *there's no holding things back*. But that's only the tip of the iceberg. Every twenty minutes or so thereafter, Bear needs more paper.

In our early years hunting together, I didn't always carry toilet paper. In those days, if I had to go, I'd gather up some leaves and make do. As I've aged, I've learned to go afield better prepared, not only for my comfort, but for Bear's, as well. Scavenging around for suitable leaves, then delivering them from upwind when he's already in the middle of relieving himself got old. Nowadays I carry a full roll of toilet paper in my pack, just for him.

Whenever Bear and I are together, I handle and prepare all the food. I figure if he has that many bowel problems after all the years his immune system has been exposed, my body wouldn't stand a chance against the microorganisms crawling around on his unwashed hands.

Besides bowel problems, Bear also has foot problems. I recall the time some years back when I mentioned that his feet would feel and smell much better if he followed my example and cared for them properly. At the time, I was thinking more of my own comfort than his.

At camp following an afternoon of scouting, I took off my dirty, wet socks and tennis shoes and wiped my feet thoroughly with a damp, soapy washcloth. Bear sat nearby with a quart of dill pickles eating one after another while complaining about the poor deer-sign we had seen.

After rinsing my feet, I said, "Hey Bear, why don't you wash your feet off for a change?"

He mumbled something under his breath, while I walked over to the creek near camp and dipped my feet in the cool, clear water.

Two minutes later, Bear plopped down at water's edge nearby, ripped off his stinking shoes and socks and dunked his fungus-infested feet in the water. The water turned milky at once.

"Even the giardia couldn't survive that," I thought. I jerked my feet out and dried them off. While I applied baby powder to my feet, Bear pulled his still-stinking feet out of the water and put his damp, reeking socks and shoes back on without bothering to dry his feet first.

The next day, when we went to ford the creek at the same place we had crossed the day before, about two hundred feet below our camp, I spotted over a dozen dead trout lying along the banks. I haven't suggested any foot care since.

In the old days, Bear weighed in at about 180 pounds. Now he weighs over 300. With all that extra weight, he doesn't get up and down the hills as easily as he used to, and sweat just pours off of him. On our last elk-hunting trip, after spraying urine all over himself, he asked to take a drink from one of my canteens.

"You mean to tell me that you're packing five pounds of elk pee but you aren't carrying any water?" I asked.

"I had to cut back on something. Besides, I figured if I ever got *too* thirsty…"

Wesley Murphey's books make great gifts!

See back of this page to order Wesley Murphey books-

Also Available soon on Amazon Kindle.

Get more information and order more of Wesley Murphey's books at **lostcreekbooks.com**. Credit cards accepted. Or order through your local book store.

Rob and Wes with step-mother, Rosella. Dexter Lake crappies 1969.

Lost Creek Books
15789 Deedon Road
La Pine, OR 97739

email: lostcreekbooks@netzero.com
website: lostcreekbooks.com

_____Cut here_____

Quick order form for Wesley Murphey books

Fiction:	Price	#books	Ext.Price
A Homeless Man's Burden	$14.95	____	_____
Trouble at Puma Creek	$14.95	____	_____
To Kill a Mother in Law	$14.95	____	_____
Girl Too Popular	$12.95	____	_____

NonFiction:			
Blacktail Deer Hunting Adventures (avail 8-2013)	$13.50	____	_____
Conibear Beaver Trapping in Open Water	$12.00	____	_____
Trap Otters, Beavers, Raccoons... (avail 8-2013)	$12.00	____	_____
Fish, Hunt and Trap a Little Volume One	$13.50	____	_____
Fish, Hunt and Trap a Little Volume Two	$13.50	____	_____
Fish, Hunt and Trap a Little Volume Three (4-2014)	$13.50	____	_____

(Plus total shipping regardless of quantity) $3.50

Total Price _____

Send check or money order to address at top of page. Be sure to include your name and address. A phone number should be included with large orders.